Software
Reliability
Guidebook

Software Reliability Guidebook

ROBERT L. GLASS

Computing Specialist
Boeing Aerospace Co.

Prentice-Hall, Inc., Englewood Cliffs, New Jersey 07632

Library of Congress Cataloging in Publication Data

Glass, Robert L 1932-
   Software reliability guidebook.

   Bibliography: p.
   Includes index.
   1. Computer programs—Reliability. I. Title.
QA76.6.G57 1979 001.6'425 79-10966
ISBN 0-13-821785-8

PRENTICE-HALL INTERNATIONAL, INC., *London*
PRENTICE-HALL OF AUSTRALIA PTY. LIMITED, *Sydney*
PRENTICE-HALL OF CANADA, LTD., *Toronto*
PRENTICE-HALL OF INDIA PRIVATE LIMITED, *New Delhi*
PRENTICE-HALL OF JAPAN, INC., *Tokyo*
PRENTICE-HALL OF SOUTHEAST ASIA PTE. LTD., *Singapore*
WHITEHALL BOOKS LIMITED, *Wellington, New Zealand*

Contents

3. RELIABILITY TOOL AND TECHNIQUE MENU, TECHNOLOGICAL   27

Preface

Software reliability has been a neglected field. Some emphasis has been placed in recent years on management to achieve reliability, and the measurement of reliability, but technology to achieve reliability has progressed little in the same time period.

That situation is changing. Software implementors and purchasers of software, particularly the Department of Defense, are beginning to insist on reliability as a requirement of delivered software. This guidebook is a survey of technological and management techniques, written as a menu. Each item in the menu is evaluated, examples of use are given, and references are provided for further study. Recommendations for achievement of software reliability are also provided.

The guidebook is intended to be useful for all application areas and sizes of software projects; special emphasis is placed on the problems of large projects, such as those of military/space applications and massive interrelated data bases.

The reader is expected to be a software manager or technologist or student who has a basic understanding of what software is, but whose knowledge of reliability concepts is either rudimentary or has not been updated to include recent developments. It should be particularly useful to the consultant who wants to present reliability concepts to a software organization concerned about the reliability of its products; as a supplement to a university-level course in software engineering; and as on-the-job retraining material for experienced software people.

ACKNOWLEDGMENTS

The author wishes to thank the following people for their role in helping this guidebook evolve from an idea into a published reality:

1. Contributing authors Paul L. Williams and Paul P. Howley. Williams wrote significant portions of the material on management reliability techniques, management planning, documentation, and estimating test completion—and part of the material on modeling and simulation. Howley wrote the sections on software quality assurance and configuration management. Without their help, the section on management techniques would have been thin indeed!
2. Ted Biggerstaff and Roger Scholten, who contributed both ideas and paragraphs full of ready-to-use material (on proof of correctness and the software life cycle, respectively).
3. Joan Bateman and Ray Turner, for their ideas and motivational support.
4. The many reviewers who contributed their time and constructive criticism.
5. The patient contributors and reviewers who saw their ideas blended into a writing style and a set of judgments sometimes different from their own.
6. And all the creative thinkers in the world of software reliability who did the original work that made a compilation of these techniques possible.

DEDICATION

This book is gratefully dedicated to all of the above, and to my friends and intimates who persevered past my compulsion to make this book come into being, and continued to like me anyway.

ROBERT L. GLASS

Software
Reliability
Guidebook

One

The Concept of
Software Reliability

1.1 INTRODUCTION

"What are the standards of reliability I expect? Isn't it much the same as you expect when you buy an airline ticket? How would you like it if an aircraft manufacturer's customer engineers replied in the following vein:

" 'Take courage, Widow Robinson, it was only the engines that conked out. The body and wings were in perfect shape. Anyway we don't make engines, so it wasn't really our fault.' "

" 'Members of the Inquiry Board, the plane behaved perfectly all week. Just a loose connection with the main fuel tank in the middle of the Indian Ocean for three minutes. It had passed all the pre-flight diagnostics.' "

" 'Ladies and Gentlemen, we request your patience at this time. Owing to an absolutely unthinkable and unforeseen problem, we can't get the new wings on properly. We hope you will find your enforced sojourn in Thule to be an unexpected pleasure.' "

"Well, why is this so ridiculous? Why do you expect so much

1

more reliability with an airplane than with a computer system? They aren't any more expensive. They are much more difficult to pilot. They are not kept in a special environment.''

''I say that the only reason is that airplane customers regard degrees of reliability as unthinkable, while computer system customers do not. And the reason why they don't is that they've been knocked on the head so often that they are incapable of clear thought on the matter. Well, my head is made of concrete, my vision is quite clear, and I am as stubborn as a Missouri mule. It is just as intolerable to allow the collection of gadgets we call a computer system to admit of unreliability as it is to allow the collection of devices we call an airplane to admit of unreliability.''

Those pungent thoughts on computing reliability, spoken over eight years ago by a computer center manager for a large user corporation,* are as true and incisive today as they were when they were first written. Computer system reliability in general, and software reliability in particular, is considered by most of us to be acceptably imperfect.

It is the purpose of this guidebook to discuss whether that state of affairs is necessary and what can be done about it.

1.2 DEFINITION OF TERMS

Sometimes it seems that the reliability field has more terms than it does tools. In this section, the most common terms in the field are defined so that a firm foundation is laid for their subsequent use. In some cases, these definitions are not without controversy. However, the definitions used here are felt to match most common usage.

1.2.1 Reliability

Reliability is defined, for the purpose of this guidebook, as the degree to which a software system both satisfies its requirements and delivers usable services. (This distinguishes reliability from *correct-*

---

*Robert A. Worsing, then Director of Systems Administration and Computing for the Boeing Commercial Airplane Division. This is an excerpt from internal speeches Worsing made at the invitation of IBM's field services and Control Data's marketing organizations in the 1968 time period. Worsing is currently Vice President, Development and Operations, Computer Sciences Corp.'s Data Service group.

ness, which is defined as the degree to which the requirements are satisfied.) Note that a system may satisfy all its requirements and still not perform usably (e.g., in a compiler the object code generated for one case of an IF statement may be incorrect or grossly inefficient, yet all other cases perform satisfactorily and the explicit requirements are satisfied), or a system may perform usably and not satisfy its requirements (e.g., implementation of processing for one set of input cases may be omitted, but the remainder of the program performs satisfactorily). (This definition is based on "The Influence of Software Structure on Reliability," *Proceedings of IEEE International Conference on Reliable Software, 1975;* Parnas. It is not universally accepted without controversy, especially by those who consider "reliability" and "correctness" to be synonyms.)

Reliability is a subset of a broader concept, *quality.* Quality software, in addition to being reliable, is also concise, consistent, efficient, maintainable, portable, and understandable. Some would also add that it is produced on schedule and within budget.

The remaining terms in this section deal with ways of achieving reliability.

1.2.2 Verification and validation

Verification and validation are processes for determining and improving the reliability of computer software; *verification* determines that the software functions properly alone, and *validation* determines that it functions properly in a total system environment (and therefore includes an evaluation of the software requirements themselves).

1.2.3 Certification

Certification is the sanctioning of the reliability of computer software by an authorizing agency.

1.2.4 Test

Testing is the process of executing computer software in order to determine whether the results it produces are correct.

1.2.5 Debug

Debugging is the process of isolating and correcting errors. Debugging and testing are often treated as being synonymous; however, debugging may involve inspection and other manual processes as well as testing, and debugging is generally considered to precede the formal (acceptance) portion of the testing process. Note that a debugged program is *thought to be* bug-free; subsequent formal testing and production usage often demonstrate that this was not the case.

1.2.6 Inspection

Inspection is the process of examining computer software and related material for correctness.

1.2.7 Checkout

Checkout is the process of improving implemented computer software for delivery and customer usability. It includes code quality improvement as well as error removal. Testing, debugging, and inspection are checkout methods.

1.2.8 Performance test

Performance testing is the process of demonstrating that computer software satisfies execution-type requirements, such as sizing and timing.

1.2.9 Acceptance test

An *acceptance test* is the set of formal processes that determine whether the software end product is acceptable to its customer.

1.3 CURRENT PRACTICES IN RELIABILITY

Software reliability has been the neglected urchin of computing. Everyone agrees that reliable software is a desirable end goal, but too little progress has been made toward improving it in the last 10 years.

This is partly due to the fact that many contracts for software production and delivery contain no dollar motivation for providing reliability. In fact, the opposite may be true; the fact of unreliable software has led to the practice of follow-on contracts for software maintenance, and thus unreliability is in a sense rewarded.

None of this should be taken to imply that totally reliable software is just around the corner, given the right contractual shove. Software production is a complex, thought-intensive task, made more complex because (for all its flaws) difficult problems migrate toward software solutions because hardware is less flexible.

Still, there is a great need for increased emphasis on reliability tools for the software craftsman. Although there has been improvement in the management aspects of reliability—design reviews, test plan documentation, configuration management, and quality control are largely steps in the right direction, and all have matured significantly in the last 10 years—the technician has had less significant help in doing his job over the same era, yet the product whose reliability needs improvement is largely fashioned by his hands. The fact that source language debug concepts (see Section 3.4.2.1) have not been made widely available, for example, when at the same time the merits of coding in high-level language have been virtually unquestioned, shows how badly out of synch the support for reliability technology has been with respect to (for example) productivity technology.

There are indications that this neglect will end. More computing research funding is being channeled toward reliability tool development. As maintenance costs become intolerable, government officials, among others, are sounding the cry for better-quality software. Ways of making the contractual instrument work in behalf of reliability are being studied, and will undoubtedly result in stiffened reliability requirements on delivered software.

However, reliability is an elusive goal. Although it is painful to admit, 100% software reliability is generally acknowledged to be beyond the state of the art. The complexity of software structure, and the combinatorial mathematics of breaking down that structure into small enough units for rigorous analysis, will probably keep that goal beyond the state of the art for some time.

The current approach to software reliability improvement, acknowledging the elusiveness of the ultimate goal, is incremental improvement. Tools, techniques, and disciplines are developed, each of which carves out an additional percentage improvement in the reliability of software using them.

What follows is an attempt at taxonomy of those tools, techniques, and disciplines. Following this menu of reliability technology is a set of recommendations for selecting from the menu for any particular software development task. Readers who are short of time may wish to read only the recommendations, but they are urged to review at least those elements of the taxonomy which seem applicable to the task at hand.

It is important to distinguish here between the achievement of reliability and the measurement of reliability. This guidebook focuses on the former. Reliability measurement of software is controversial; whole books have been written on the subject, but some software specialists still feel that the use of such traditional reliability concepts as "mean time between failure" are meaningless for software (because when it fails, it is always an inherent design/implementation failure, never a fatigue failure). Section 4.4 of this guidebook deals with the measurement of reliability; but the *entire* guidebook deals with achieving reliability.

The term *state of the art* is often used in what follows. The term is ambiguous. In the context of these pages, it should be taken to mean "common software practice." This is not the same as "the latest software developments," another definition of the term frequently used.

Quantitative estimates of the cost of tools and techniques are also often included in what follows. These estimates are derived from educated and experienced intuition, nourished at times by the costing of such tools and techniques as part of implementation or proposal efforts. Such numbers as "tool A costs X thousand dollars," or "technique B increases implementation costs by $Y\%$," should be taken not as totally accurate numbers but as ballpark estimates. And it should be remembered that dollar figures are valid as of the publication date; inflationary/recessionary compensations should be made to adjust to the reading date.

Two

The Role of
Reliability in
Software
Development

2.1 INTRODUCTION

It is not only the field of software reliability that is on the move—even our view of reliability's role in the process of software development is changing.

In the past, reliability had a well-defined slot in the software developmental process. It came along right after implementation, and right before delivery. A lot of different terms and euphemisms were used to describe the reliability process—checkout, debugging, testing—but everyone knew what it was, how you did it, and when it happened.

It was the sometimes-chronic unreliability of software produced in this way that caused the development process to be looked at again. Data from an occasional software experiment began pointing to the design phase as a major source of errors. Programmers always had known that unstable requirements were a major cause of revision-driven errors. Gradually, it became apparent that *all* phases of the software development process needed to be subject to reliability review. Because of that history, software reliability is now a field that spans the entire software development process.

It is the purpose of this section to describe that software development process, and to show the interaction of reliability technology with development technology. That interaction, in fact, is the basis for the organization of this guidebook. Individual sections that follow in Section 3, for example, show reliability technology applicable to specific development stages.

2.2   THE SOFTWARE LIFE CYCLE

The process of software development and use has in recent years come to be referred to as the *software life cycle.* There are some good things and some bad things about that name.

The good thing is that a new emphasis is placed on all phases of the development process, including the software maintenance phase. Especially in cost considerations, realism demands that the development of software be considered more than a coding process. When all of the life-cycle time and cost factors are measured, coding of software in fact ranks near the bottom, and maintenance ranks at or near the top. Thus the phrase "life cycle" puts in perspective an outlook that had become skewed.

The bad things are that the name is not intrinsically meaningful when applied to software. There has been a tendency, in recent years, to (1) bemoan the low cost effectiveness and reliability of software, and (2) borrow concepts and tools helter-skelter from other fields in an effort to correct that problem. Some of the borrowing has been good and worthwhile; but not all of it. The term "life cycle" is an example of the latter. "Life cycle" implies something that is born, matures, and dies. Hardware, for instance, is created, fitted into a process, used, and worn out. But software does not die, and software does not wear out. Software becomes obsolete, and in that sense it "dies"; but its life expectation is dependent on external factors much more than its innate nature. This is a semantic quibble, however; "life cycle" as a term serves a useful purpose; therefore, it is a term worth using.

The life cycle of software is made up of several phases. What those phases are called is not universally agreed upon, but what they actually involve is commonly understood.

The first phase, in this guidebook, will be called *requirements/ specifications.* Elsewhere it may be called *systems analysis.* It is the phase where the problem is being understood and defined. A solution to the problem may evolve during the requirements/specification phase, but it is held in check pending complete understanding of the problem. Only then should a solution be consciously considered; its representation is then stated in terms of a specification for a software system, and that specification is the primary output of the requirements/specification phase. Perhaps the greatest hazard during this phase is the temptation to define a solution to part of the problem, ignoring the hard parts or those that are ill-defined. Succumbing to this temptation leads to inadequate design and implementation, which in turn leads to revised requirements and major modifications (or, in fact, to "death" of the system). Modification of existing software is probably the greatest plague of the software profession. It is difficult, costly, and frustrating. Many a program has been thrown away and rewritten because it was "unmodifiable." Thus well-thought-through requirements and specifications are vital to both the quality and reliability of the software they define.

The second phase is the *design phase.* It is time to translate the problem and its requirements specification into a conceptual solution, a blueprint for the actual solution or implementation that will follow. Computing-specific considerations are made: What computer? Which of its resources, and how much? What language? What modules? What sequence of functions? What data structures? What else? All these ingredients are dumped into the specifications-defined pot and stirred into a workable and specific plan. The primary output of the design phase is a design representation. It may take the form of words, flowcharts, decision tables, program design language, or any number of other popular or semipopular choices. One of the greatest problems in the design phase is knowing when to quit. There is a growing concern that traditional design approaches have been inadequate, quitting too soon, leading to inadequate solutions and a high number of design errors. The opposite concern is equally valid. Grinding a design deeply into the nitty-gritty implementation details wastes time and money, since it is at best a replication of the implementation process. A solution to this dilemma —vital to both the reliability and cost aspects of the software life cycle—is still dependent on specific situations.

The third phase is that of *implementation.* The design solution of the previous phase is translated into a computer-readable, computer-processable form. The computer software takes actual shape and becomes an executable, problem-solving entity. The intricacies and vagaries of the computer and the language are met head on and dealt with. Separate building blocks are constructed and appended to the growing whole. There is the illusion—or perhaps the reality—of crafting a hold-it-in-your-hands product, a Stradivarius capable of making the computer play fine music. And the greatest risk is carelessness. Computer programs are a mass of fine details, many of them interrelated and many of them brain-busters in their own right. There is the ever-present danger that carelessness can turn a Stradivarius into a K-Mart toy.

The fourth phase is *checkout.* Checkout is the process of examining and playing the Stradivarius to see if it meets its standards. Checkout is playing Sherlock Holmes to a frustrating series of program-flaw-caused "crimes," sifting through clues to identify (and rehabilitate) the criminals. Checkout is a game played with the program and the computer, where the programmer has only one choice—win (although "how you play the game" is also important from a reliability point of view). Checkout is seeking programming errors, seeking design errors, questioning questionable requirements, and putting the final polish on the soon-to-be-usable computer program. The great hazard here is impatience. Checking out a program must be a painstaking process of trying out all the requirements, all the structural elements, and as many of the combinations of logic paths as common sense and cost/schedule considerations permit. The temptation is to stop short, declare the program fit, and ship it off to its users. The dimensions of this error are monumental. A disgruntled user, one who mistrusts a computer program, may never regain that trust. And a computer program can die from lack of trust.

The fifth phase is *maintenance.* Poor old, much-disliked maintenance. Maintenance is the process of being responsive to user needs—fixing errors, making user-specified modifications, honing the program to be more useful. Programmers tend to avoid mainten-ance activities—they lack the spark of creativity. If design is the quarterback of software glamor, implementation and checkout are the remainder of the offensive team, and maintenance is the work-aday defense—vitally necessary, but usually unheralded. It is ironic that the maintenance programmer, who may be the most important customer relations factor in the software life cycle, is often the least senior, least capable person on the staff. Which brings us to the greatest hazard of maintenance—ineptitude. A finely tuned Stradi-varius can be reduced to high-quality fireplace wood by a ham-handed maintainer. All the good of all the previous phases can be undone in the glamorless, unheralded world of maintenance. Recent and future trends in computing will undoubtedly stress the correction of this problem.

Figures 2.1 through 2.5 graphically illustrate some cost, error, and reliability aspects of the life cycle. They show maintenance as the dominant phase on a cost-analysis basis, design as the dominant phase on an error creation basis, acceptance test and maintenance as dominant phases on an error discovery basis, and some interphase reliability methodologies. These figures are especially interesting in that they display some decidedly nonintuitive data.

Several studies have been conducted on actual costs of the various phases of the software life cycle. Although there are variances between them, Figure 2.1 presents a roughly accurate breakdown. Note the dominance of the maintenance phase.

REFERENCES

1. "The High Cost of Software," *Practical Strategies for Developing Large Software Systems,* Addison-Wesley, 1975; Boehm.

2. "The Economics of Software Quality Assurance," *Proceedings of the National Computer Conference, 1976;* Alberts.

3. "Characteristics of Applications Software Maintenance," UCLA Graduate School of Management, 1976; Lientz, Swanson, and Tompkins.

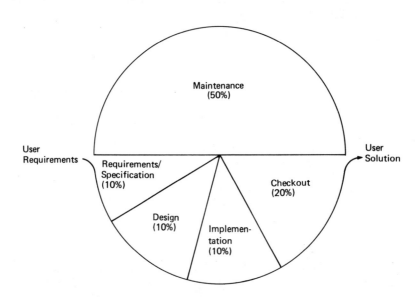

Figure 2.1   Software Life Cycle: Costs per Phase

Studies have also been conducted on when during the software life-cycle, errors are generated. These studies typically start after the requirements/specification phase, assuming that the specification is a baseline against which errors are measured. They also typically measure only errors detected after integration or acceptance or delivery. Design errors dominate the picture. Other major sources of minor errors are programming language syntax, and the complex job control language of one leading hardware vendor (one study estimates that the latter accounts for two-thirds of all implementation phase errors).

REFERENCES

1.   "Software Design and Structuring," *Practical Strategies for Developing Large Software Systems,* Addison-Wesley, 1975; Boehm.

2.   "Reliability Measurement During Software Development," *Proceedings of the AIAA Conference on Computers in Aerospace, 1977;* Hecht, Sturm, and Trattner.

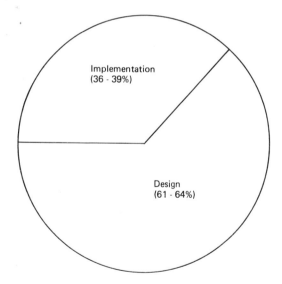

Figure 2.2   Software Life Cycle: Error Sources per Phase

Studies show that errors typically are not detected until very late in the software life cycle. The predominant number are found during or after the acceptance test.

REFERENCES

1. "Software Design and Structuring," *Practical Strategies for Developing Large Software Systems,* Addison-Wesley, 1975; Boehm.

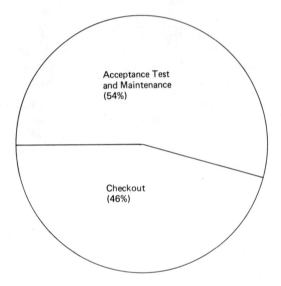

Figure 2.3   Software Life Cycle: Error Discovery per Phase

The cost of fixing an error rises dramatically as the software progresses through the life cycle. Maintenance costs (per error) are enormous.

REFERENCES

1. *Software Acquisition Management Guidebook,* Software Maintenance Volume, System Development Corp., TM-5772/004/02, Nov., 1977; Stanfield and Skrukrud.

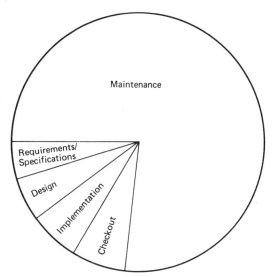

Figure 2.4   Software Life Cycle: Per Error Fix Cost per Phase

Of the many software reliability techniques discussed in this guidebook, several are especially appropriate as bridges between the life-cycle phases. They are shown in Figure 2.5.

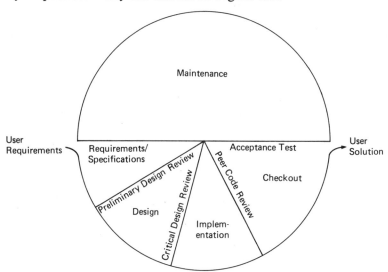

Figure 2.5   Software Life Cycle: Interphase Reliability Techniques

2.3 RELIABILITY IN THE LIFE CYCLE

It has already been emphasized that reliability considerations should impact all phases of the software life cycle, not just checkout. With a definition of those phases of the life cycle clearly in mind, let us now talk about the ways in which reliability and those phases interact.

But first, let us define the concept of a software reliability technologist and discuss in general the approaches he is able to employ as he moves through the software life cycle, the Johnny Reliabilityseed of software, sowing correctness as he moves.

First of all, Johnny Reliabilityseed may actually be Janey Reliabilityseed. There are no sexual distinctions in software reliability, and the he's and him's of this book should be taken as generic and not chauvinistic.

Second, Johnny Reliabilityseed may be a member of the software development team, performing reliability work along with his other life-cycle activities, or he may be a member of a software quality assurance organization, dedicated only to quality and reliability tasks. The discussion that follows places no organizational requirements on the tasks to be performed.

There are a lot of specific techniques and methodologies which Johnny Reliabilityseed may employ as he goes about his work. Specifics of those techniques are discussed later in this guidebook. But in general, they may be categorized in four ways—test, analysis, demonstration, and inspection. These categories are defined as:

1. *Test.* Execution of the code under controlled conditions to generate and record realistic performance data. These data will be evaluated to ascertain compliance with requirements.
2. *Analysis.* Logical or mathematical processing of analytical or empirical data under defined conditions. Analysis may include evaluation of internal control logic functions, numerical and statistical performance of algorithms and equations, sizing and timing parameters, core memory allocation, priorities, and so on.
3. *Demonstration.* Execution of operational or functional capabilities before qualified witnesses. Instrumentation

and data recording normally will be provided indigenously by the elements being demonstrated.

4. *Inspection.* Examination or observation of the computer program against the applicable documentation to confirm compliance with specified requirements. Inspection may consist of visual examination for the presence of desired characteristics or the absence of undesired characteristics.

Armed with these capabilities, Johnny Reliabilityseed now moves into the various phases of the software life cycle.

2.3.1   Requirements/specifications

During the initial phase of software development, analysis of software requirements is conducted. Johnny Reliabilityseed will participate in the review and analysis of the system specification and computer program specification to ensure that the functional and interface requirements are correctly allocated to software. This review is conducted to verify that only those system requirements that can be realistically accomplished by software are allocated to computer programs. Verification of requirements during this phase will also assure that all requirements, documented in the specification, are traceable to the system specification and that the requirements are clear, complete, correct, and testable. It is necessary to begin with valid, testable requirements and specify quantitative criteria that can be measured to determine success, rather than general requirements. Testable requirements are those which are specific and unambiguous, with a clearly identifiable result when they are met: for example, specify that the accuracy should be "within $\pm 1\%$" rather than "sufficient to meet mission requirements."

A requirements matrix, which correlates all software requirements with the system requirements and the software/hardware and software/software interface requirements, should be prepared and included in the specification. Each software requirement will also have a reliability requirement established and documented to define the method of verification and the success criteria. There should be a one-to-one correspondence between the software requirements and the reliability requirements. This should also be included in the requirements matrix. Johnny Reliabilityseed will review this matrix to assure completeness.

2.3.2 Design

During this phase of software development the requirements are translated into a design representation. Johnny Reliabilityseed will participate in design reviews, analyzing the design to verify that it accurately reflects all software requirements. Algorithms and equations may be verified by mathematical analysis or by simulations. There should be traceability between design and its driving requirements.

Reviews and analyses conducted to verify the design include the following:

1. Review all external functional interfaces (e.g., with system equipment and communication links). Review word lengths, message formats, storage available within the computer, timing, and other considerations which were established in the specification.
2. Review all internal functional interfaces. Analyze word formats, transfer rates, and so on, for incompatibilities.
3. Analyze critical timing requirements of the system as they apply to the software to ensure that the proposed computer program design will satisfy them. Review estimated running time for adequacy.
4. Review the structure of the program as a whole with emphasis on allocation of requirements to components, storage requirements and allocations, operating sequences, and design of the data base.
5. Review the program interactions with human performance requirements.

2.3.3 Implementation

During this phase of software development, Johnny Reliabilityseed will review and analyze the code to verify that it correctly implements the design. Inspection of the code is conducted to verify that the coding process has not introduced errors. Verification can be performed by manual code reviews and inspections and by the use of automated software tools. Verification of the code should be conducted during the coding process to detect errors as early as possible. This verification should also be performed after the code is produced and during maintenance or updating of the code.

2.3.4   Checkout

Most of the software reliability effort is in the checkout phase and this is traditionally where Johnny Reliabilityseed has his largest and most readily accepted role. Since checkout can account for 40 to 50% of the software development (predelivery) cost, this is also an area where Johnny Reliabilityseed should concentrate his efforts. It should be noted that the early effort of software verification, during requirements analysis, design, and coding, is aimed at the early detection and correction of software problems or errors and thus at the reduction of problems detected during checkout.

Verification accomplished by testing and other checkout methods should demonstrate that the results of executing each equation, each logic branch, each input/output statement, and so on, satisfies the specification requirements. Owing to the complexity and large size of computer programs, and the budget and schedule constraints, it is almost impossible to test, or execute, all possible combinations of input data or paths that the program is capable of executing. The results of testing are therefore subject to a good deal of uncertainty. Supplementary checkout techniques, such as peer code review and structural (static) analysis, are also used by Johnny Reliabilityseed for this reason.

A good test program probably requires the development of a test plan to define all levels of testing. For a complex computing system, several levels of testing will be required to verify that all requirements are met: unit testing will be conducted to verify that individual components have been properly coded and that they satisfy corresponding software design requirements; integration testing will be conducted to verify that software/software interfaces between computer program components and with the executive program are satisfied; computer program testing will be conducted to verify that hardware/software interface requirements are properly implemented and software requirements contained in the specification are satisfied; and finally system testing will be conducted to demonstrate that the operational system meets the performance and design requirements of the system specifications. Should top-down development methodology be used, the line between unit and integration testing becomes less distinct; the essential principles outlined here, however, still hold.

Johnny Reliabilityseed's checkout activities are also concerned with the adequacy of the test cases, the conformance of test conduct and test results with test procedures, the control of the configuration tested, the timely reporting and correction of all software deficiencies, and the tracking of corrective action. The test plan is reviewed to ensure that the planning and test case definition are adequate and that appropriate levels of testing are planned. The test plan should identify the schedules, test methods, and success criteria as well as all required support facilities, equipment, software, and personnel. It should include plans for testing at both nominal and extreme conditions. The test procedures are reviewed to assure that they clearly define the test objectives, test inputs, expected results, data recording requirements, and data reduction requirements. Traceability between verification requirements and individual tests should be documented.

Following informal testing, formal or acceptance testing should be conducted to demonstrate software adequacy to the customer. Prior to the start of a formal test, a test readiness review meeting should be held. Any problems uncovered during this review will prevent errors and delays from occurring during the conduct of the test.

Johnny Reliabilityseed should assure that the conduct of all formal tests will be subject to monitoring to verify that the test procedures are being followed, test results are accurately recorded, and any discrepancies between actual and required performance are reported and dispositioned. Johnny Reliabilityseed will track all software discrepancies discovered in the testing process until a retest demonstrates their proper resolution. The results of all testing are published in test reports.

2.3.5 Maintenance

Verification of software requirements continues throughout the software life cycle. It does not end when the software has been accepted by the customer and is in the operational phase. Whenever changes are made to the computer program, either for enhancements or to correct problems, they should be verified. Johnny Reliabilityseed will participate in the review of changes and their impact on software requirements. He will also assure that adequate retesting is accomplished to verify that the computer program still meets its requirements and that documentation is updated along with the corresponding code. Additionally, he will design and monitor an error tracking system, to enable the researching of specific error status and the watching of error trends to judge software status.

2.4 SMALL VERSUS LARGE PROJECTS

The discussions in this guidebook touch on a difficult topic in several different places. That difficult topic is the distinction between small projects and large projects. It is the purpose of this section to confront the distinction and underscore the ways in which it affects the remaining material in the guidebook.

It is a mistake to minimize the importance of size. A large project may well require an entirely different set of both technological and managerial methodologies than a small one.

Size is defined later (in Section 5, that on recommendations). To give you a preview, however, a project will be called small if it involves 5 or less programmers, medium if it involves 6 to 29, and large if it involves more than 30. It is entirely possible to disagree with this definition, since it is relatively arbitrary; but it is much less possible to disagree with the impact of these distinctions. To put these sizes into some degree of perspective, however, a few applications, together with the category into which they fall, are cited: commercial data processing report generators or some support software tools (e.g., assemblers, linkers, etc.) are usually small projects; a modern rapid transit software system or more complex support software tools (e.g., a compiler for a major language such as PL/1 or JOVIAL) are medium-sized projects; and an avionics control system for a new technology aircraft (e.g., the E-3A radar aircraft) or an extremely complex support software tool (e.g., the operating system for the IBM 360/370 series) are large projects.

Communication is often the bane of the large project. Communication between people, communication between software modules—each of these requires special consideration and special solutions.

On the other hand, lack of resources can be the bane of the small project. Dollar resources, to procure adequate support tools. People resources, to explore peripheral but task-related functions. And this lack of resources forces its own set of considerations and solutions on the small project.

In the software world, the environment of the small project is pretty well understood. There are lots of them, for one thing. They are easy to simulate in the research environment, for another. It is *not* true that all the problems of the small project world have been solved; but the existing problems are at least fairly well understood.

But the large (and even medium-sized) project is another matter. Problems of how best to staff, to organize, and to support a large project must be solved. How can the emerging technologies be used in the large project environment? For example, the following technological and managerial software reliability methodologies, discussed in Sections 3 and 4, are not at all well understood in the large project environment:

1. Top-down programming.
2. Proof of correctness.
3. Symbolic execution.
4. Chief programmer team.

The situation is more complicated than its impact on emerging methodology, however: even traditional methodologies are not well understood in the large project environment. In particular, interfacing and integration of software are downright traumatic on large projects.

It has been argued that large software project development methodology is a totally different intellectual exercise than small project development. If this is indeed true, a whole new set of methodologies should be developed to support the large project environment. In general, this has not been done. To date, the solution to the large project dilemma has largely been one of increased formality—formally defined schedules, formally defined and scheduled reviews, formally specified and reviewed documentation, and a formal system of checks and balances. With respect to the latter, several layers of organizational complexity may be superimposed over the basic software development organization. Split off into separate organizations, for example, may be the processes of quality assurance, configuration control, product test, system integration, subcontract management, systems analysis, and design. This solution, of course, increases the problem—if communication was the bane of the large project before, it is made worse by the formality and checks and balances necessary to keep it all under control. Thus the difficulties of a large project increase by more than a linear relationship to the size of the project.

To make matters worse, all the formality begins to exact a toll on the freedom and creativity of the individual large project participant. To make the large project manageable, individual differences tend to be subordinated to a common set of requirements. If, for example, a design is to be completed by November 12, those who design more rapidly tend to have nothing to do after completion, and those who design more slowly tend to work voluntary overtime to catch up. Schedules not only must reflect a level of common mediocrity, but tend to enforce it. "Routinization," the process of forcing a mass of programmers into a lockstep schedule, emphasizes the "peas in a pod" alikeness of technologists formerly known more for their idiosyncracies. And new technologies are looked to more as standardizers of large group performance than as tools to assist the creative craftsman. In this kind of environment, for example, structured programming is lauded more for its limitation on individual control constructs (e.g., "forbid the GOTO") than for the positive benefits of the improved control constructs (e.g., "hooray for the IF-THEN-ELSE").

It would be nice to conclude this discussion with a set of recommended solutions to the dilemma. Unfortunately, there are few, if any. One proposed solution—use of a small team of skilled software craftsmen instead of armies of more mediocre people—simply will not work. There are already far more problems awaiting programmers than there are programmers available to staff them. And the skilled craftsmen are the first of the needed horde snapped up and put to work. There simply are not enough skilled people, let alone unskilled people, to go around.

Probably the only possible right answer is the development of improved tools specific to the large project world. One author proposes a "module interface language" to help define the complex interfaces between large numbers of modules. A cross-reference lister that works at both the system and the compiler levels would be another useful tool. The energies of the research segment of the software field are desperately needed to explore the needs of the large project. Unfortunately, researchers, like the rest of us, tend to work where it is easy to work rather than where they are really needed.

(In the 1940s, there was a rash of "little moron" jokes analogous to the elephant jokes of a later era. "What are you looking for?" the little moron was asked in one such joke. "I lost my keys," he replies. "Where did you lose them?" "Over there." "Then why are you looking here?" "Because the light is better." The light is also better for the researcher investigating the problems of the small project environment. It is difficult to create and study a real 30-person project inside ivy-covered halls.)

REFERENCES

1.   *The Mythical Man-Month,* Addison-Wesley, 1975; Brooks.

Describes the experiences of and insights resulting from the development of the operating system for the IBM 360. Recommends small teams organized in specific ways, project workbooks, change-oriented organizations, effective tool usage, and a plans and controls group among other methodologies for assisting the large project manager.

2.   *Programmers and Managers,* Springer-Verlag, 1977; Kraft.

Laments the "de-skilling" of the technologist in the large project environment. Notes the "routinization" of the tasks performed previously by "creative and perhaps eccentric" people.

3. "Programming-in-the-Large Versus Programming-in-the-Small,"
    IEEE Transactions on Software Engineering, June, 1976; DeRemer
    and Kron.

Defines the need for a "module interconnection language" (MIL) for the large project environment. Sees the MIL as enhancing reliability through improved project
management, technological communication, design support, and design documentation. Shows examples of use.

4. *Practical Strategies for Developing Large Software Systems,* Addison-
    Wesley, 1975; Horowitz.

A collection of papers with the common theme of solutions to large system problems. Two papers on each phase of the life cycle (except maintenance) and on the
management of large projects. Well-chosen authors (Boehm, Schwartz, Royce,
Wolverton, Brown, Stucki, Bratman).

5. "Impact of MPP on System Development," RADC-TR-77-121,
    1977; Brown.

Describes the modern programming practices (MPP) used on a huge (up to 400
people) software development project (an anti-ballistic-missile system) at TRW.
Evaluates those practices by polling technically knowledgeable participants. Finds
they improve quality but have a less obvious impact on costs and schedules.

6. "Viking Software Data," RADC-TR-77-168, 1977; Prentiss.

A frank and detailed description of the problems and successes on the software for a
major space system. Viking required 1783 man-months and 278,575 source cards
over a 4-year period.

Three

Reliability Tool
and Technique Menu,
Technological

The technology of software development is somewhere on a path between its origin in the small shops of elitist craftspeople and its potential "promised land" of automated, assembly-line-like factories.

There is a serious question as to where on this path we really are. Some claim that automation is just around the corner and hail each new technology development (such as structured programming) as evidence that we are drawing closer. Others say that not much has really changed (Herb Grosch says software is a "cottage industry") and that software folk are really artists, ad-hocking their way to nonscientific software solutions.

There is also a serious question as to where we *should* be going on that path. Is automation of software development really either feasible or desirable? All evidence indicates that the process of software development is very thought-intensive. Can we automate other thought-intensive processes, such as bridge design or electronic engineering?

There is, however, a point of commonality for the widely divergent views. Whether the software technologist is an artist/craftsman, or a plug-compatible assembly-line worker, he needs tools. The tools and techniques these technologists use determine to a major extent both the quality and quantity of the work they produce.

Tool development in the broad field of software development is a long-established and recognized practice. Compilers, loaders, libraries, . . .—the list is long. Tool development in the narrower field of software reliability, on the other hand, is relatively recent. Not much has happened over the past decade until now.

With the advent of immensely more complicated software systems (some software folk said that a reliable Safeguard antimissile system could not be built, for example), the focus of attention in the software world has swung to reliability. Many new software reliability tools and techniques are now available. Whether the reader is new to the software field, or an old CPC coder from the archives of computing history, he will find that there is much to be learned in the recently and rapidly expanding field of software reliability.

The list of technological tools and techniques that follows is critical to the producer of reliable software. For ease of reference and understanding, the list is structured in the order of where in the software development cycle the tool or technique is used.

REFERENCES

1.   "A Glossary of Software Tools and Techniques," *Computer (IEEE),* July, 1977; Reifer and Trattner.

Divides software tools into six categories—simulation, development, test and evaluation, operations and maintenance, performance measurement, and programming support. Lists 70 types of tools, categorizing them as above.

2.   "Testing Large Software with Automated Software Evaluation Systems," *IEEE Transactions on Software Engineering,* Mar., 1975; Ramamoorthy and Ho.

Lists and describes automated software tools. Summarizes reports of operational experience on some (FACES, AIR, ACES, PACE).

3.1 REQUIREMENTS/SPECIFICATIONS TECHNIQUES

The quest for reliable software continually moves its attention earlier and earlier in the software development cycle.

"If the testing goes badly, it is because of faulty implementation," begins this line of reasoning. "If implementation is faulty, it may well be due to poor design," it continues. "And if the design is inferior, perhaps the requirements and/or specifications are at fault."

The chronology of investigation into techniques of software reliability has proceeded pretty much as described in the preceding paragraph. Thus the newest and least developed area of software reliability is in the realm of requirements and specifications. However, research efforts are thriving in this area, and a great deal has been published in recent years on this technology. It is easy, therefore, to talk about the promise of increasing software reliability through requirements/specifications techniques, but it is still very difficult to demonstrate results.

The problem is further complicated by a blurring of definitions. Most software people would agree that requirements are a statement of the criteria that a computer program must satisfy; specifications are a representation of those requirements in human-readable form; and design is a "how-to" statement of the specifications such that they can be implemented. But these loosely worded understandings do not translate well into practice. Need a requirements statement be massaged at all to make it into a specification, for example? And where is the dividing line between specifications and preliminary design? Even the literature is fuzzy on these points.

And in some circles, "specification" is taken to mean any definitive document (the "maintenance manual," for instance, is referred to as the "computer program development specification"). This guidebook will use the more specific definition of specification, limiting it to the expression of requirements for a total program and its modular breakdown, as it is commonly used in the literature.

The key to distinguishing specification efforts from design efforts appears to be the following, however: a specification for a software system tells *what* the software does or should do, and design tells *how* it will do it. That level of definition, at least, is generally accepted.

Another blurring factor is the lack of understanding of differences between various kinds of computing applications. The needs of a specification technique for a data processing application, for example, may be significantly different from those for a scientific application. Whereas the requirements gathering process for the former is highly people-oriented and generally accomplished by specialists called "systems analysts" with a business-oriented set of skills, the requirements gathering for the latter is much more mathematical in nature and is often performed by the programmer or a "mathematical analyst" or both acting as a team. Obviously, the resulting problem statement and software specification will heavily reflect the nature of the application and the background of the requirements gatherer. Where the blurring occurs is in the advocacy of requirements/specifications techniques without regard for the intended application area. Just as there is no one best programming language for all software implementations, there is probably no one best requirements/specifications technique independent of application area.

One factor that is too often ignored in attempts to advance the requirements/specifications technology is the apparently elementary problem of identifying a sufficient set of requirements. The state of the software art is such that the requirements themselves are typically inadequate; it is not their representation, but their existence, which is the most pressing problem. Requirements definition for commercially procured software is sometimes incredibly naive. One compiler procurement specification, dated 1977, sets the following requirements for the output produced by the compiler—"the compiler shall output symbolic assembler language statements as specified in the computer programming manual." Notice how many questions are left unanswered by this requirement:

1. Is there any printed output (listings, etc.)? What should it look like?
2. Are there to be diagnostics? How many, under what circumstances, and what kind?

3. Does the compiler interface with any other software, such as a loader? Should the interfacing file format match requirements levied by the other software?

4. Precisely what kind of symbolic assembly language is to be produced—that which feeds into an assembler, or that which feeds directly into a loader? (Incredibly enough, in this specification the latter was meant, even though the obvious interpretation was the former.)

5. Are there any optional outputs, such as cross-reference lists, maps, or object code lists?

6. What quality requirements are imposed on the output code? Optimizations? Global? Local? Or will just any old code that works do?

Obviously, the requirements for just this one facet of this one compiler program comprise a problem demanding more than cursory attention.

The task of defining the requirements for a reasonably complex piece of software may well deserve the "systems analysis" job title defined by the business data processing folk. Determining which of the requirements for a total system are applicable to its software is the beginning task, and a sometimes awesome one in its own right. Specifying a sufficiently definitive envelope of requirements to define the quality of the software itself taxes most state-of-the-art computer people. Not just the functions the software performs and the criteria for performing those functions (how big? how fast?) must be defined, but such detail-level considerations as product limitations must be identified and spelled out. More than one piece of software has been discarded or rewritten because, although it functioned as it was expected to function, it had insufficient capacity to handle real-world input loadings.

Perhaps what is needed to enhance the reliability expectations of requirements/specifications at this infantile state of the art is simply checklists of the kinds of things that should be included. This approach would obviously have prodded the compiler output specifier of the previous example to come up with more than simply "produce assembler code." Until these elementary problems are solved, more sophisticated solutions may simply further blur the already blurred problems of the requirements/specifications realm.

In spite of the blur, however, there is material of potential substance in this area. The sections which follow describe tools and techniques that may prove useful to those faced with the problem of documenting requirements and specifications.

3.1.1   Requirements/specifications language

Requirements and specifications have traditionally been stated in natural language. To be sure, the form of that natural language has been rather unnatural, heavily flavored as it is with sentences beginning "Thou shall" or "Thou shall not." But be that as it may, even with a mild "unnatural" flavor, natural language is the way things are done.

It is probably natural for the computer scientist to turn to language design as an area of possible promise. For one thing, requirements and specifications must be stated quite carefully since they usually form the Bible upon which all subsequent software decisions are based. But for another, computer scientists like languages. Given a choice of problems to solve, the typical computer scientist may well choose the one that allows him to define a language.

This somewhat facetious look at the evolution of requirements/ specifications languages may or may not be unfair; only time will tell. However, most work currently reported in the literature on requirements/specifications technology is in the language realm. And, to its defense, since the end result of the software development process involves use of a programming language, it makes sense to state the first representation of the problem in a manner that might conceivably evolve into the coded representation itself. In fact, as may be seen in the references in this section, the requirements/specifications language may indeed be a subset of an actual programming language.

The question of language formality must be dealt with. It is an area of controversy. There are those researchers who insist that formality is a necessary ingredient of a requirements/specifications language, citing the rigor of that approach and the possibilities for automated consistency checking. And there are those who swear by informality, citing the constraining nature of formalism and the immature state of the art, which could make formality premature or even dangerous. Time and subsequent developments will eventually resolve this controversy. Some advocate a middle ground, at least in the meantime, suggesting that formalism be used where appropriate, supplemented as necessary by informality.

State of the Art in Requirements/Specifications Languages

Requirements/specifications languages are still in the research phase. Few, if any, industrial computing installations use the technique. Natural language is still the commonly accepted method of representing requirements and specifications.

Cost of Requirements/Specifications Languages

Meaningful discussion of the cost of requirements/specifications language usage is difficult, owing to the newness of the concept. Informal languages will probably cost no more than traditional techniques once the learning cost increment is past; more formality may lead to added cost. If an automated consistency checker is used, acquisition costs may be significant; up to $75,000 at professional salaries and industrial overheads, depending on availability.

Example of Requirements/Specifications Languages

You have been asked to design and implement a program to simulate the playing of a game of baseball as a management training tool for a school for baseball managers. Because the customer has been relatively unclear in the requirements he presented you, you feel it would be wise to write a clear specification of the problem he wants solved, both as a baseline for further development efforts and as a check on your understanding of his wishes. You elect to use a specification language to do so.

Since your computing installation has no standard specification language, you decide to use an informal one of your own design.

After a survey of the literature on specifications languages, you define the following available language forms:

```
SPEC
    INPUT (list of inputs)
    OUTPUT (list of outputs)
    ACTIONS (list of verbs and explanations)
    CONSTRAINTS (list of bounds on actions)
END-SPEC
```

For input, based on your understanding of the customer's wishes, you have a roster of players, each player accompanied by his statistical data (batting and fielding averages, etc.). You also have the ability to name a starting lineup and to change that lineup as the game proceeds. For output, you will print the result of each pitch (ball and strike count, type of pitch, etc.), an end-of-inning summary, and an end-of-game summary. The game will be played interactively by two managers-in-training, or one manager against the computer; each manager may make lineup changes (per baseball's normal rules) after each pitch, if he wishes. The playing of the game will rely heavily on a random-number generator whose results will be weighted by individual player statistics to determine what happens on each pitch (curve, fastball, . . ., hit, walk, error, . . .). You have misgivings about naming the existence of the random-number generator at the specification level—it is more of a "how" statement than a "what" one—but you anticipate that your customer will want to know that particular design detail, and it is a fundamental enough part of your notion of the problem that you decide to include it.

With this background, you represent the specifications as follows, and submit them to both your customer and a few carefully selected peers for review.

```
SPEC
    INPUT (ROSTER OF PLAYERS:
        PLAYER, PLAYER STATISTICS;
        STARTING LINEUP (IN BATTING ORDER):
        PLAYER NAME, PLAYER POSITION;
        LINEUP CHANGE:
            REMOVED PLAYER NAME, REPLACEMENT PLAYER
            NAME, POSITION;)
```

OUTPUT (PITCH-BY-PITCH RESULT (LINEUP CHANGE
    ALLOWABLE): TYPE OF PITCH, BATTER ACTION;
    END-OF-INNING SUMMARY:
    SCORE OF GAME, HITS-RUNS-ERRORS-
    LEFT ON BASE;
    END-OF-GAME SUMMARY:
    SCORE OF GAME, HITS-RUNS-ERRORS-
    LEFT ON BASE;
    PLAYER STATISTICS UPDATE;)
ACTIONS (GENERATE RANDOM NUMBER
    FOR EACH PITCH;
    APPLY PLAYER STATISTICS TO RANDOM NUMBER;
    DETERMINE TYPE OF PITCH AND BATTER ACTION;
    TRACK CONTENT OF ROSTERS, LINEUP, AND BASES;
    TRACK SCORE AND STATISTICS;)
CONSTRAINTS (NORMAL RULES OF BASEBALL;)
END-SPEC

The customer is reasonably satisfied with your spec. However, he reminds you that the user-manager needs to be able to access updated player statistics interactively in order to make lineup changes, and that you have not included "ALLOW LINEUP CHANGE" under "ACTIONS" even though it is provided for under "INPUT." You make that change in your spec language representation and proceed to the design phase. "How to," rather than "what to," now becomes your problem.

REFERENCES

1. "The Evolution of Specification Techniques," *Proceedings of the 1977 Annual Conference, Association for Computing Machinery;* Wasserman.

    Outlines the goals and trends in specification techniques. Identifies reliability and customer communication breakdown as the driving factors. Names several representative languages and discusses when they are most applicable.

2. "GYPSY: A Language for Specification and Implementation of Verifiable Programs," *Proceedings of an ACM Conference on Language Design for Reliable Software, 1977;* Ambler, Good, Browne, Burger, Cohen, Hoch, and Wells.

Discusses a specific Pascal-based language designed to provide both specification and implementation capability. Criteria for language definition—including verification, incremental development, real-time and other design goals—are discussed. An example of the use of GYPSY is presented.

3. "Formal Module Level Specifications," *Proceedings of the 1977 Annual Conference, Association for Computing Machinery;* Buckles.

Describes SSL (software specification language), a preliminary design tool for module-level specification. Language forms are named and discussed. Advantages of usage are described.

4. *IEEE Transactions on Software Engineering,* Jan., 1977.

Contains a collection of papers on requirements analysis. Covered concepts include Softech's Structured Analysis and Design Technique (SADT), as described by Ross; the University of Michigan's Problem Statement Language/Problem Statement Analyzer (PSL/PSA), by Teichroew and Hershey; TRW's Requirements Statement Language and Requirements Engineering and Validation System (RSL/REVS), by Bell, Bixler, and Dyer; and others.

3.1.2   System modeling and simulation

Modeling is the act of constructing or designing an entity that usefully represents the modeled object or process. *Simulation* is the process of causing a model to interact with a real or simulated environment in such a way as to gain information about the properties of the simulated system. For example, building a scaled-down replica of an aircraft is modeling; placing it in a wind tunnel to determine flight characteristics is simulation.

One of the principal benefits of modeling is in the opportunity for requirements and design verification. Suppose that you are responsible for building a real-time computer system for controlling the carburetion in an automobile engine. You know that your computer problem is relatively simple, except for a complex set of interactions with other engine elements. Because of the tricky interfaces, you decide to model the engine and the role your computer system plays in it. In that model, you parameterize some of the design decision elements of your computer system so that you can easily modify them and measure their impact on the overall engine system. Similarly, out-of-range conditions and other stress situations can be simulated and their results analyzed. By better understanding the total system, you may modify your design and perhaps even your specification to better mesh with reality.

Modeling and simulation may be accomplished in a variety of ways in the software world. Basically, any simulation can be coded using any valid software methodology. However, there exist some language systems with special tools for simulation building. For example, GPSS (General-Purpose System Simulator) is a language designed specifically for simulation development; and Simscript and Simula add simulation capabilities to standard programming languages (Fortran and Algol). (Simscript has evolved from its Fortran base into a language in its own right.) Thus the technology for simulation construction is well advanced.

Modeling and simulation language systems provide a wide variety of facilities for modeling continuous and periodic or stochastic (statistically distributed, random) discrete functions. The ones that are useful for simulation of data processing functions and software usually provide some or all of the following features:

1. *Hardware host model.* A method for representing various hardware features of single processor or multiprocessor computer systems.
2. *Control flow model.* Capability for establishing the desired execution sequence for the various software units of the system modeled.
3. *Data flow model.* Capability for defining the generation and evolution of data blocks in the model.
4. *Interface model.* Facilities for modeling the inputs of the data processing system, based on data rates, their periodicity or statistical distribution, and I/O capacity parameters.
5. *Performance model.* A means for assigning core storage requirements and processing times to modeled code segments.

A general-purpose modeling language is of little use without companion facilities for running the model. These facilities are usually implemented as relatively independent but related support and utility computer programs. In addition to the usual operating system software, some of these programs which commonly support a simulation language include:

1. *Compiler.* This translation program converts the model description in the simulation language into executable code.

2. *Input/scenario generator.* This facility is often incorporated
    into the compiler as a part of the overall model description
    process. A scenario (or event sequence) represents the
    external environment of the simulation system.
3. *Simulator operating system.* This software facility provides
    the job control, run-time executive, and monitor routines
    necessary to execute the simulation routines and collect
    data during the run.
4. *Data postprocessor.* Postprocessor capability is required to
    extract the desired data from the information recorded
    during a simulation run. This program takes data collected
    by the simulator operating system and selectively evaluates,
    edits, and outputs it into a format specified by the analyst.

In spite of the sophistication of modeling and simulation
technology, there are some problems in its use:

1. *Divergence.* Software tends to be very difficult to model
    effectively, since many of the quantitative parameters cannot
    be estimated with confidence during the earlier phases of
    the development process. Evolution of design concepts
    that are not reflected back into the model also promote
    divergence.
2. *Quality of results.* Where empirical, rule-of-thumb methods
    or crude mathematical models can be used to obtain a
    "good-enough" estimate of the characteristics of the soft-
    ware, there is very little incentive to build an elaborate
    model .
3. *Cost.* The design effort and computing resources needed to
    build, check out, and run a large simulation can use up
    large amounts of manpower, computer time, and schedule
    lead time. Resource-short projects are justifiably wary
    of such expenditures unless the payoff can be quantitatively
    demonstrated.

As a result, simulation may be categorized as a powerful but expensive tool.

State of the Art in System Modeling and Simulation

Modeling and simulation have been among the applications of computing since the beginnings of the field. Languages especially designed to support simulation started to become available in the early 1960s. The notion of simulation as a tool to evaluate software requirements and design has evolved in parallel with the broader uses of simulation. Simulation, therefore, is a well-established concept. Because of the above-mentioned problems, however, its use as a software requirements/design aid is limited, and it is used only on systems prepared to accept the attendant problems and costs.

Cost of System Modeling and Simulation

The development of a model, and the cost of executing it, are both considerable. It is not possible to be quantitative without considering specific simulations.

Example of System Modeling and Simulation

You have been asked to construct a fault-tolerant computer system for the control of carburetion in a formula racing automobile. Your job is similar to that mentioned earlier in this section, except that there is now heavy emphasis on a fully reliable fuel system, and less emphasis on costs. To assure fault tolerance (the owner and driver would both feel badly and be irritated if your carburetor failed one lap before the checkered flag dropped on a world championship race with $50,000 prize money), you decide to use a triply redundant system of processors—that is, the same software runs continuously in three computers, and if their results differ, they vote to determine which one has failed, dropping it from further use.

Because of the reliability requirements and the complexity of the application, you convince your customer to spend the extra money needed to simulate the system. You elect to use GPSS as the modeling language, and you begin gathering data on automobile and engine performance to serve as the basis for the model. The engineer who designed the car and the engineer who designed the engine have most of the information you need, and the skilled mechanics in the owner's shop can estimate the rest. You model the engine at the level

of each piston stroke and corresponding electrical system and carburetor actions, and stress the functioning of the software-hardware
system controlling the carburetor.

You choose to define "transactions," the units upon which GPSS
operates, as pulses through the engine's electrical system and
elements of the fuel flow. The transactions move through blocks you
have specified for them—the gas tank, the fuel lines, the fuel pump,
the carburetor, the battery, the electrical connections, the
distributor, and the ignition chamber. In each of these blocks, a
series of actions you specify impacts the transactions. Such functions as throttle pressure, heat and humidity, and car attitude are applied to define the actions. When the model is executed, the transactions flow through the blocks of the system, and a record is made
of the resulting modeled actions. Interactions between the transactions and the computer hardware/software system are also tracked.

The model, when run, verifies that your software as specified will
do the job. However, you discover a fuel slosh problem which will
only occur on hard braking and report that result to the owner. The
fault is corrected, both in the system and in the model, and the subsequent runs of the model make the upcoming championship season
look promising.

REFERENCES

1. "The Modeling and Analysis of Supervisory Systems," Stanford
    University, STAN-CS-72-271, 1972; Riddle.

Presents a modeling scheme and associated method of analysis for use during the
design of large software systems. Shows examples of applicability to correctness
analysis.

2. "Description of the Functionally-Oriented System Simulation (FOSS)
    for Software/Hardware Design," Boeing, D180-18617-1, 1976;
    Scallon.

Describes FOSS, a system that couples a formal specification language to a Fortran
precompiler so that the specification can form the definition of a simulation. Discusses the use of FOSS, particularly as it applies to real-time multiprocessing
systems. Proposes the concept of automated evolution of the model into actual
code. Illustrates FOSS usage via an example.

3.1.3 Requirements/specifications traceability

It is one thing to define requirements and write specifications. It is quite another to keep track of them once the deed is done. In a system of any size, tracing requirements as they are interpreted into design and then into code can be a major problem. What design elements or code satisfy requirement "A"? What requirements are this design element or code intended to satisfy? The answers to those questions can be quite illuminating, especially if a requirement changes or the value of a section of design or code is questioned. Perhaps even more important, questions about the existence of code for particular requirements can quickly be resolved.

One way of tracking requirements is to note the driving requirements for each design element or section of code in the design representation or as comments in the code listing. Additionally, a master requirements tracking document, perhaps part of the eventual Maintenance Manual, can summarize for each requirement where the related design elements or code sections may be found. Even better, the elements related to a particular requirement may be "threaded" from one element to the next (e.g., each element not only identifies its driving requirements, but the "next" and perhaps even "previous," element related to each requirement). Then the master requirements document need only point to the first element on the "thread."

One company—Computer Sciences Corp.—has formalized this requirements threading process, deriving several fringe benefits from doing so. All system requirements are threaded from the relevant system inputs through the processes that manipulate them to the resulting outputs. The technique is especially useful in design verification and in forcing the early definition of interfaces between threaded system elements. In addition, *threads* have proven useful in the organization and management control of large software projects. Threads that are functionally related in a practical way are gathered into what are called *builds,* where a build is an element of the total software system that can be implemented more or less autonomously from the rest. A build is constructed and integrated as an entity, prior to total system integration. A *build leader* is responsible for all technical decisions related to a build. And overseeing the entire

41

Threads/Builds organization is an automated *threads management system,* which tracks progress of threads and builds as a vehicle for management control and customer status reporting.

Whether this degree of formality is needed or not is a valid question, but in any case the tracing of requirements/specifications through a design and implementation has significant merit, especially in large and complex systems.

State of the Art in Requirements/Specifications Traceability

The process described above is more often espoused than used. It is not often found to be common practice. However, the concept is supported by most managers of large software projects.

Cost of Requirements/Specifications Traceability

Most of the elements of requirements traceability involve a discipline more than they involve a tool. As a result, the actual cost is minor. However, a management commitment and a traceability process definition must be made prior to use of the technique.

Cost of an automated threads management system is more significant, since the software for the tool must be implemented. However, this cost should be under $75,000 (at professional salaries and industrial overheads).

Example of Requirements/Specifications Traceability

You elect to employ traceability in your baseball simulation program, partly because your customer has indicated that he wants close visibility on your implementation efforts.

Each requirement in your requirements language specification given in Section 3.1.1 is assigned an identifying designation, to simplify the job of recording all implications of the requirements. All input requirements, for example, are assigned the key first letter I, and each requirement is then given a mnemonic name (for a larger system, a number, although less meaningful, might be more practical). I-ROSTER, for instance, defines the roster of players input requirement and I-CHANGE the requirement to allow the input of lineup changes. Similarly, A is used as a key first letter for actions, and A-PITCH defines the requirement to generate a pitch of a defined set of characteristics (fastball, forkball; thrown by lefthander; etc.)

As the design is formulated and emerges in design representation form, the driving requirements are noted as part of the representation, as parenthetic expressions for each element of the design. And as your design is programmed into code, the requirement mnemonics are carried through as comments within the code itself. Successor and predecessor references for each noted requirement are also encoded and noted. The documentation of the program, as well as its coded respresentatives, also reflects the thread notation. Progress reports to your management, too, are thread-specific; thus threads and their references permeate the software at every level of its existence.

The system pays off when your customer decides to modify the way in which the user-manager is allowed to make lineup changes. Each software element which must be changed is attached to the requirement by a threaded list, and the impact of the change is quickly defined, scoped, and implemented. The "nuisance" of recording apparently extraneous information has paid off technically as well as managerially.

REFERENCES

1. "Software Production Data," RADC-TR-77-177, 1977; Carter, Donahoo, Farquhar, and Hurt.

    Describes research performed by Computer Sciences Corp. to assess the effects of "modern programming practices" (MPP). Defines threads, builds, and the threads management system, and assesses their actual use on various projects. Compares MPP with IBM's definition of structured programming (SP). The impact of elements of MPP and SP on the software life cycle, and on common error types, is estimated.

3.2 DESIGN TECHNIQUES

Software design may well be the portion of the software life cycle least amenable to tools and methodologies, and most desperately in need of it.

Design is a thought-intensive task. As such, it is difficult to define approaches to design which are applicable to some broad spectrum of software builders. The spark of creation, which most vitally needs to be ignited during design, appears to have different combustion points and different burn rates for different people. One person's catalyst may well be another's mental straightjacket.

And yet the design phase is critical to the quality and reliability of the product that results. It may be possible to produce a poor implementation from a good design, but it is seldom possible to produce a good implementation from a poor design. Design, then, is a make-or-break phase for software construction.

In the overall picture of the software life-cycle process, design is preceded by requirements definition and specification preparation. The designer, therefore, should have a fairly firm problem definition to work with, and be able to concentrate on methods of solution rather than methods of problem definition. But in practice, this is often not the case. Those who have a problem to solve often are unaware of the detailed problem specifics, and the entire requirements–specifications–design cycle is all too commonly an iterative process. Thus the designer not only needs thinking skills, but a high tolerance level, flexibility, and some gift of prophecy. Again, it is difficult to develop tools or methodologies to enhance these traits.

Because of the above, the state of the art in design tools is rudimentary, and evolution is slow.

Historically, the software design phase has blurred more-or-less indistinctly into the implementation phase. This may be necessary, in the case of particularly unusual or difficult problems for which design efforts must be supported by experimental implementations. From a reliability point of view, however, the transition from the conceptual design phase to implementation should be treated like the pouring of cement—it may well be wise to check the forms one last time before proceeding.

Design is the process of converting a hopefully rigorous problem statement into a plan for an algorithmic-specific or a computer-specific solution. The designer looks at a problem from the viewpoint of solution techniques played against the realities of capabilities of computing machines and software technology. His output can range anywhere from a declaration of infeasibility to a blueprint for implementation. He must include in his design some room for expansion, anticipating future requirements. His needs in this process include a way of approaching the problem, a sounding board to review his thinking, and a convenient and readable representation of his results. These areas are addressed more specifically in the material that follows.

3.2.1 Design approaches

If someone gave you the requirements and specifications for an elephant and asked you to design one, you might wonder where to start, particularly if you had never seen an elephant-like animal. Do you start with the trunk because it is the most unusual feature, or the feet because you understand that problem best, or the brain because it controls the rest of the animal? Or all of the above, because you need to understand the whole problem early on?

The software designer has the analogous problem. How do you address the totality of a problem whose specification may well contain a thousand tiny details? Solving this problem is vital; many a piece of elephantine software is really a dog with a trunk tacked on.

Obviously, the solution must involve breaking the specification up into manageable chunks; the question of how to do this is answered in several different ways by what follows.

REFERENCES

1. "Comparing Software Design Methodologies," *Datamation,* Nov., 1977; Peters and Tripp.

Presents and analyzes five different design approaches. Evaluates the approaches based on trial usage. Concludes that no single approach is valid for all problems, and that "designers produce designs, methods do not."

3.2.1.1 TOP-DOWN DESIGN

Top-down design is a design approach that begins with the most abstract description of the functions of a system. From this single highest-level system description, successively more detailed subsystems are designed. This process is repeated until the level of design is sufficient for coding. The result is a hierarchic or tree-structured design. Each level must consist of a complete description of the system before the next level of finer detail is built.

The value of top-down design is that it provides manageable levels of complexity at each stage of the design process. Additionally, at each stage the relation of each constituent to the other is known. Hopefully, via such an organized approach, there is early visibility into design problem areas, and avoidance of focusing on low-level details until their overall context has been decided.

Top-down design is also sometimes referred to as "hierarchic decomposition"* because of the cascading nature of the process.

State of the Art in Top-Down Design

Given that the problem of a design approach is really one of chopping a software specification into manageable and digestible chunks, one obvious and successful approach is to identify and separate the functions to be performed. Most software designers tend to work in this way. Top-down applies an ordering to that approach.

There is, however, a fundamental question raised by top-down design concepts; what *is* the most abstract description of the system? If the specification is written properly, it is clearly identified; if it is not, however, the designer is left with the problem of believing in top-down design but being unable to locate the top.

For example, one design of a real-time operating system clearly labeled by its designer as "top-down" began with the real-time computer's interrupt structure as the top. It is no more apparent that that particular aspect of the real-time system is its "top" than, say, the user services which the operating system is to provide. In this case, the design had the aura of top-down design but not necessarily any of its characteristics. (This is not to say that such a design is wrong, just that it is not clearly top-down.)

---

*For an interesting philosophical (non-computing-oriented) discussion of hierarchic systems, see *The Ghost in the Machine,* App. I, Macmillan, 1967; Arthur Koestler. Rules, strategies, equilibrium, and disorder are among the aspects of hierarchies discussed. The "open hierarchical system" is discussed and advocated.

There is one other problem with top-down design as described above. If the hierarchic decomposition is to occur one level at a time before passing to the next level, it may well delay the detection of feasibility problems lurking at a low level. It is true in the software world that serious problems occur at all levels of detail, and it is not uncommon to flush them out only when the bottommost detailed implications of a process are dealt with. A hierarchic structure may, of course, crumble if one of its lowest-level elements collapses.

However, this does not change the fundamental fact that top-down is a good approach. The alternative may be to bog down early in the details of a system while neglecting its overall structure. The problem of lurking low-level problems is usually solved by an iterative top-down process, in which the implications of low-level problems are dealt with in a redesign starting down from the top.

Note that top-down design and top-down programming, discussed elsewhere in this material, are different concepts. Top-down programming is one approach to implementing a design; there are others. There *are* those who interrelate the two concepts—design and implementation are to occur in tandem, in top-down order. Few actually follow this philosophy, however. The current emphasis is usually on separating design and implementation further, not intermingling them.

Example of Top-Down Design

You have been asked by an apparently serious manager to build an elephant simulation program. (Actually, the simulator is one of a series commissioned by a local veterinary school to demonstrate the relationship between animal subsystems and behavior.) Your customer hands you a good specification for an elephant, including characteristics of its simulator, and you decide to employ the top-down approach.

First, you do a hierarchic decomposition of the elephant simulation's component parts. At the top, you put the behavioral aspects of the simulation. Subsidiary to that are each of the subsystems whose impact on behavior you wish to analyze. And each of those subsystems, in turn, is broken down into its significant components.

In graphic form, you end up with this design (it was developed downward, one horizontal level at a time):

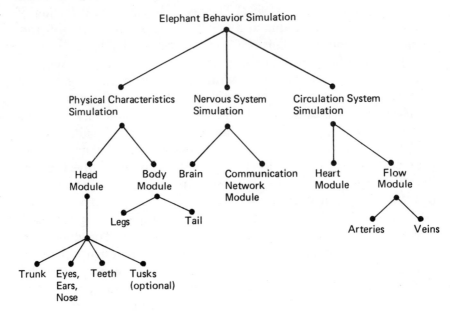

Figure 3.1   Elephant Behavior Simulation

From the point of view of the total simulation, each design element represents the model representation of that physical component of the elephant. For example, the "brain" element represents a block of the simulation through which neurological pulse flow will be measured, and the "heart" another such block, which processes circulatory transactions.

You have managed to segment the originally elephantine task into a manageable set of individual modules.

REFERENCES

1.   "Structured Design," *IBM Systems Journal,* Vol. 13, No. 2, 1974; Stevens, Myers, and Constantine.

Discusses modular breakdown and the interrelationships between modules. Defines steps necessary to design a structure. Considers data structures in overall design structure.

2. *The Mythical Man-Month,* p. 143, Addison-Wesley, 1975; Brooks.

Characterizes top-down design as "the most important new programming formalization of the decade." Describes the refinement steps leading to a top-down design.

3. "Top-down Development Using a Program Design Language," *IBM Systems Journal,* Vol. 15, No. 2, 1976; VanLeer.

Relates program design language (see Section 3.2.3.3) to top-down design, showing an example of the top-down process leading to a program design language representation.

3.2.1.2 DATA STRUCTURE DESIGN

Contrasted with the functional approach of top-down design, which tends to decompose specifications into functional components, is the *data structure design* approach. This approach focuses on the structure and flow of information rather than on the functions performed.

The value of data structure design (sometimes called the *Jackson method*) is that it attempts to narrow the choices of the designer—as was shown in the preceding paragraphs, there is sometimes ambiguity in defining the top of a top-down design. However, the data structure designer has a more clear-cut series of tasks to perform—define the data structures, identify data flow, define the operations that enable data flow.

As with top-down design, this approach focuses on the task of breaking up the design into manageable chunks. The chunks, in this case, are data-oriented rather than function-oriented.

One problem that can arise with data structure design is the *structure clash,* where the data structures to be processed by a program are in some sense not synchronized (e.g., the input file is in sequence by employee-name, the output file is to be sorted on salary rate; or in the input stream is a continuous stream of characters, with logical records asynchronous to physical records, while the output stream is a more traditional logical-records-blocked-into-physical-records structure). Solutions to the clash problem are defined in the references—the creation of an intermediate file, or the conversion of one structure processor into a subroutine for the other, are among the possible solutions.

State of the Art in Data Structure Design

Data structure design is an approach fairly commonly used in data-oriented programs such as business data processing applications (e.g., producing reports from and updating data bases). However, it has only recently begun to achieve attention in .the computing literature. As a formal notion, it is still being explored.

Cost of Data Structure Design

As with other design methodologies, there is no acquisition cost to data structure design, and usage costs are at present not possible to quantify.

Example of Data Structure Design

Once again, you have been asked by an apparently serious manager to build an elephant simulation program. In this case, you elect to employ a data structure design approach.

First, you identify the simulation data structures. There are scenario input data, which define the overall actions of the simulation; transaction data, which defines the elements to flow and queue in the simulation; event queue definitions themselves; and report output data, which contains the simulation results. For example, the transactions will include (as before) neurological pulses and circulatory elements, and the actions will include brain events and heart pulses. Printed outputs will show the dynamic and final states of the queues, events, and overall behavior. Figure 3.2 shows a summary diagram of the data structures.

Next, you design the form and content of each of the structures shown. In so doing, you are forced into a deeper understanding of the specific data items which will make up your simulation. The layout of the input and output formats may seem fairly mundane, but the makeup of event queues and the impact of elephant elements on them begins to introduce you to the depths of the physical problem.

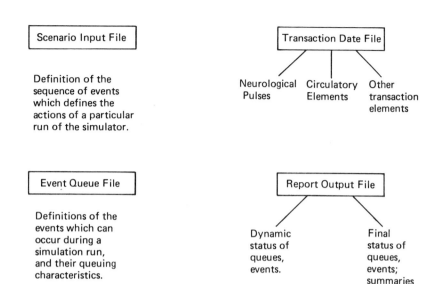

Figure 3.2

Then you design the flow of information between the structures. The scenario, for example, is used to initialize the event queue; transaction flow through the simulated events is defined; and event results are reformatted into output reports. Now you are really coming to grips with both the data structure and the functional elements of the simulation.

Finally, you define the operations necessary to cause this flow of information to occur. You have effectively concentrated first on the simulator's data instead of the elephant's structure.

REFERENCES

1. "Basic Program Design—the Jackson Way: An Example," *Proceedings of the 1977 Annual Conference, Association for Computing Machinery;* de Lavigne.

A contrast is drawn between functional decomposition and data structure as design approaches via a census data problem example. Limitations of the functional approach, and methodology of the data structure approach, are discussed. A complete bibliography of Michael Jackson-authored articles and books is presented.

2. *Principles of Program Design,* Academic Press, 1975, Jackson.

Takes a problem-oriented approach to design concepts—each concept is followed by a problem solution illustrating the concept. Problems are taken from the data processing realm, and sample code is in COBOL. Data structure design is stressed.

3.2.2 Design reviews

The designer of his first computer program (or elephant) may begin to feel a little insecure around the edges as his design efforts progress. (The designer of his 100th program often feels that way, too.) Unless he has been afflicted with a severe ego problem, he will probably begin to wish that he could share his design with a few skilled and sympathetic peers, especially those who have designed similar computer programs (or animals). He may also wish that his customer would make a pass over his design, to make sure that the customer's real requirements (hopefully, reflected in the program specifications) are in sync with what he has designed.

It is to satisfy these needs that the design review was created. (It was also created, of course, so that management and the customer could better monitor the designer's progress!) The design review is an analysis of the design of a computer program conducted to determine if the proposed implementation is capable of (1) meeting specified performance, design, and verification requirements; and (2) has a high probability of successful realization within the projected schedule and budget allocated for the task.

Design reviews, especially in the government world, usually come in two flavors—the *preliminary design review* (generally referred to in the government world as the PDR), and the *critical design review* (CDR).

The PDR comes early in the design process and is an attempt to make sure that the proper design course has been set.

The CDR comes at the end of the design process and is a last chance to correct design flaws before they are cast in the concrete of code.

Design reviews can be organized in several different ways. Most commonly, one of these two approaches is used: (1) the designer makes a verbal presentation of the design, augmented by graphic aids, and the review becomes a seminar between the designer and the reviewers; (2) the designer issues a written design document prior to the review, and the reviewers submit written comments which are dealt with at the review. The first concept involves a review driven by the design; the second, a review driven by comments on the design.

The question arises: What information should form the basis for a review? One answer to that question is the following—a PDR presentation should include a computer program development plan, outlining schedule and task chronology, and a function, interface, and data structure breakdown of the problem at a fairly high level; and the CDR should include a proposed user manual, a first-draft maintenance manual (sometimes called a computer program development specification), a proposed acceptance test plan, and a complete breakdown of major functions, algorithms, interfaces, and data structures. All of the presentation material should be subjected to design review analysis.

Most important, the success or failure of a design review is dependent on people. The people who attend must be intelligent, skilled, knowledgeable in the specific problem area, cooperative, and have the time available to dedicate themselves to the review. Only the interactions of capable people can make a design review successful. The review should be chaired by someone with both authority and technical skills, and who is also able to motivate and direct the participants into staying on course. This may be the designer, his manager, or a technically knowledgeable customer.

State of the Art in Design Reviews

Design reviews, in an informal sense, have been sporadically used since the beginnings of the computing era. The more formal concept of a design review is about a decade old. Spurred on by government requirements for innovative and huge software projects, a more formal process slowly and painfully evolved. The design review is a keystone of that process.

Modern-day concepts of egoless programming, such as those presented in Weinberg's *The Psychology of Computer Programming,* fit nicely with the design review technique. The responsibility for the design, resting primarily on the designer, is at the same time shared among the design review attendees. As a result, its use, already large in the government/military sector, is on the increase in the commercial sector.

Cost of Design Reviews

It would be naive to claim that there is no cost associated with design reviews. The preparation time of the designer, especially if documents and presentation material must be written and distributed prior to the review, is a serious consideration. The time spent by reviewers, since there may be several of them, is also a cost factor.

However, on balance, design reviews save more money than they cost, owing to early exposure and elimination of design errors that might be quite costly to repair later.

There are projects, however, where the cost of the design review process is sufficiently large to consider eliminating it. On a small project, for example, lessening the formality of the design process and/or eliminating the preliminary design review (but keeping the CDR) may be cost-effective alternatives.

Example of Design Review

You have completed your elephant simulation program design, but because you have never seen an elephant, you are extremely dubious about what you have done. You ask your management (or perhaps your management asks you!) to schedule a design review, in this case a CDR. (Even if you were not ignorant about elephants, hopefully you would still see the merits of an independent design review in helping to eliminate errors early in the software production process.)

Because you want competent reviewers, you select as participants your colleagues who have just completed a camel simulation and a cocker spaniel simulation. Additionally, you invite the customer who is paying you to build an elephant simulation, and your manager.

In preparation for your review (and as part of your overall documentation task), you document the functional, interface, and data structure characteristics of the design; the simulation algorithms you have developed; draft a user manual and an acceptance test plan; and ship the CDR package to each of the attendees. Several days before the review, their comments on the CDR package arrive. You scramble to prepare a response to each comment prior to the review.

Some of the comments are trivial, dealing with typographical errors. Some are antagonistic, and your hackles rise at the cavalier way in which "your" design is "attacked." But some are extremely valuable. The comment that you have inadvertently appended the simulated trunk to the rear of the simulated body, for example, will prove very helpful in restoring design credibility once it is acted on.

The review itself is very taxing. You have been selected to chair the review, with authoritative support provided by your management. Keeping the participants moving through the comments and your responses, while at the same time allowing digressions that appear productive, requires a great deal of group discipline. Since the goal of the review itself is to reach agreement on resolution of each comment, you must be constantly mentally alert and aware of the consequences of resolutions. This requires intense self-discipline.

At the conclusion of the review, however, you are elated. A few problems have been unearthed and corrected, and your design has been stamped feasible and acceptable by knowledgeable peers, your management, and your customer.

The implementation of the elephant simulation can now begin.

REFERENCES

1. RADC-TR-74-300, Structured Programming Series, Vol. 15 (Validation and Verification Study), pp. 3-5 through 3-8 and 3-20 through 3-22, May, 1975.

Describes several aspects of a design review: selection and role of personnel; the review procedure; examples of errors to look for; and advantages and disadvantages. Review objectives, inputs, and outputs are discussed.

2. "Programming as a Social Activity," *The Psychology of Computer Programming,* Van Nostrand Reinhold, 1971; Weinberg.

Discusses "egoless programming" and individual ownership of programs. Advocates the team approach to software development and review. Uses an anecdotal approach.

3. *Reliable Software Through Composite Design,* pp. 117–119, Petrocelli/Charter, 1975; Myers.

Defines the design review as an element of the "management of design." Lists questions participants should ask.

3.2.3 Design representation

It is one thing to conceive a design in the mind. It is quite another to write it down in such a way that it is useful. Since the design must be communicated—at design reviews, as feedback for the designer himself, and eventually to the implementer—the representation of the design becomes important.

The evolution of design representations in the software world has been an interesting sequence of advocated concepts. One of the early techniques, flowcharting, evolved to a national standard status but is now under serious attack (see References, Section 3.2.3.1). Decision tables, which came along later, are useful in certain kinds of problems. A relatively new concept, the program design language, is evolving as the latest favorite. Perhaps the only valid comment to make is that design representation technology is in a state of flux.

There is, however, one area of design representation technology which has led to confusion—the need for both high-level, overview-oriented, and detail-level, nitty-gritty descriptions. Often the documented version of the design representation concentrates on detail-level information and neglects top-level considerations. In fact, it is often not only difficult to grasp the overview of a design, but there is no material that connects the top level to the detail level, even if the former is presented.

What seems to be needed is a "blueprint" approach to design representation. In blueprint technology, a top-level overview blueprint is given which identifies all subordinate, more detailed blueprints. Each successive blueprint identifies all higher-level blueprints to which it applies and all lower-level blueprints derived from it. Thus there exists a continuum of representations, each pointing to all other related representations, in a hierarchic description of the system. For the typical software design representation, this might consist of three to five levels of "blueprints." This is, however, one to three levels more than are usually produced.

It is unclear at this point in the design representation state of flux whether the same medium that is appropriate for detail-level forms is also appropriate for top-level forms. The hierarchic input-process-output (HIPO) representation, for example, argues that it is not, and provides a schemata appropriate to overview representations.

Various design representations are discussed in the following sections.

REFERENCES

1. "Software Design Representation Schemes," *Proceedings of the Symposium on Computer Software Engineering,* 1976; Peters and Tripp.

Surveys contemporary design representations. Distinguishes between global (top-level) and local (detail) representations. Discusses several concepts not included here, but omits program design language. Analyzes possible future directions.

3.2.3.1 FLOWCHARTS

A flowchart is a graphical representation of a problem design solution, using words and geometric figures to indicate function and lines with arrowheads to indicate sequence of functions.

For example, the reading of a book could be flowcharted as follows:

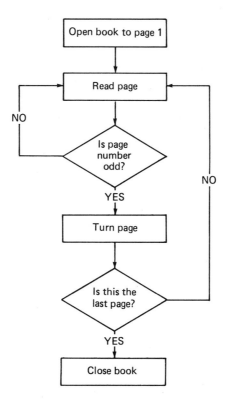

Figure 3.3

Note that actions are enclosed in rectangular boxes and questions in a diamond. Note also that two sequences result from the questions, such as "Is this the last page?" A fairly elaborate set of standards for shapes of flowchart graphics has been developed, and sanctified as a national standard.

Flowcharts assist the design process by providing the designer with a graphic representation of his design, one which makes it easy for him to see relationships and flow between design elements, in order to mentally review the accuracy of the design.

State of the Art in Flowcharts

Historically, the flowchart has been used for two totally different purposes, and considerable confusion has resulted from this state of affairs. On the one hand, the flowchart is a design aid, useful to the designer in expressing his ideas. On the other hand, the flowchart is a program documentation technique, representing an as-implemented program. Because the design aid often evolved into the program documentation, the two were often considered to be the same.

However, the goals of the two uses of flowcharts are radically different. The designer needs a visual aid that is flexible and expressive and can bend to match his thought processes. The documenter, on the other hand, is recording in flowchart form a system that already exists, and he needs representability and clarity. Further, the designer, at least in the early stages, can work with rough and dirty representations and throwaway iterations, while the documenter strives for printable quality and adherence to formal standards.

The current attack on flowchart methodology is largely, although not entirely, directed at the documentation flowchart. The flowchart as a design aid, which is the subject of this discussion, is still acknowledged generally as one reasonable alternative technique.

As stated previously, the flowchart has been used as a design representation scheme virtually throughout the history of computing. A national standard for the documentation flowchart has been established, which tends to be used in design work as well. Because many programming standards and procedures manuals still require flowcharting (primarily for documentation purposes), there is still widespread usage. However, the attack on the technique (see the References) is increasing.

Cost of Flowcharts

Flowcharts are not particularly costly to produce, although there is a requirement for the use of a graphics specialist for the preparation of document quality flows. There is a higher cost to maintaining them, caused by the difficulties of changing their fairly rigid structure. All too frequently, therefore, flowcharts are out of date. Therein lies the real cost and danger in their use. As a design aid, however, flowcharting costs are comparable to those of other design representations.

Example of Flowcharts

You have been assigned to elaborate the design for reading a book as presented earlier in this chapter. You know that the design, as shown earlier, is at best naive. As a result, you consider more deeply the process of book reading and come up with a more elaborate design as shown in Fig. 3.4.

Note that the earlier flowchart is not made entirely obsolete by the new one. Although the new one is more complete, the old one presents a good high-level overview of the process of book reading. Thus there are gradations of design representation, depending on the goal of the representation and the intended audience.

REFERENCES

1. "Flowchart Symbols and Their Usage in Information Processing," X3.5-1970, American National Standards Institute, 1971.

Presents the definition of the standard flowchart.

2. "Flowcharting with the ANSI Standard: A Tutorial," *ACM Computing Surveys,* June, 1970; Chapin.

Discusses the history and content of the ANSI flowchart standard. Illustrates using the standard at some depth, and deals with problems in its use.

3. "Experimental Investigation of the Utility of Detailed Flowcharts in Programming," *Communications of the ACM,* June, 1977; Schneiderman, Mayer, McKay, and Heller.

Describes the history of flowcharts and experiments to analyze their value. Essentially no value was found attributable to the flowchart, even in its use as a design aid.

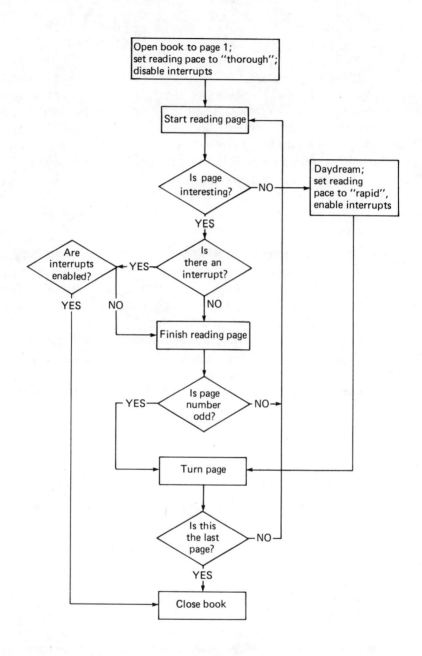

Figure 3.4

4. *The Mythical Man-Month,* pp. 167–169, Addison-Wesley, 1975; Brooks.

Debunks the flowchart; calls it "oversold," a "curse," and "obsolete."

5. "Software Acquisition Management Guidebook, Software Maintenance Volume," System Development Corp. TM-5772/004/02, Nov., 1977; Stanfield and Skrukrud.

Recommends that the Department of Defense *not* procure flowcharts with delivered software; that heavily commented and indented listings be used instead.

3.2.3.2 DECISION TABLES

A decision table is another kind of graphical representation of a problem solution, using conditions that the solution must evaluate and actions to be taken upon encountering the various conditions.

For example, the reading of a book could be represented in a decision table as follows:

Conditions				
Page = first	Y	N	N	N
First < Page < last and even	N	Y	N	N
First < Page < last and odd	N	N	Y	N
Page = last	N	N	N	Y
Actions				
Open book	X			
Read page	X	X	X	X
Turn page	X		X	
Close book				X

Each column represents a unique combination of conditions that results in the one or more actions noted in the action portion of the table.

State of the Art in Decision Tables

Decision tables have their highest applicability in logic-oriented programs that must process a great number of decisions, such as problems where numerous alternatives must be exhaustively considered. For this type of application—some business data processing programs commonly take this form—the decision table design representation may actually be converted into code via a preprocessor, such as a decision table to COBOL translator. Thus where decision tables are used, that usage is sometimes highly sophisticated. However, decision tables are not commonly used. This may be due to both inapplicability to less logic-oriented programs, and lack of knowledge of the concept.

Cost of Decision Tables

The decision table as a design representation is no more or less costly than alternative techniques, as long as it is applicable to the problem at hand.

Example of Decision Table

You have been assigned to elaborate the book reading design in a manner analogous to that used in the flowchart section. Your design becomes:

Conditions														
Page = first	Y	Y	N	N	N	N	N	N	N	N	N	N	N	N
First < Page < last and even	N	N	Y	Y	Y	Y	N	N	N	N	N	N	N	N
First < Page < last and odd	N	N	N	N	N	N	Y	Y	Y	Y	N	N	N	N
Page interesting	N	Y	N	Y	N	Y	N	Y	N	Y	N	Y	N	Y
Interrupts enabled	N	N	N	N	Y	Y	N	N	Y	Y	N	N	Y	Y
Page = last	N	N	N	N	N	N	N	N	N	N	Y	Y	Y	Y
Actions														
Open book	X	X												
Start reading page	X	X	X	X	X	X	X	X	X	X	X	X	X	X
Finish reading page	X	X	X	X		X	X	X		X	X	X		X
Turn page	X	X			X	X		X						
Close book					X			X			X	X	X	X
Daydream	X		X				X				X			
Set read rate to thorough		X		X		X		X		X		X		X
Set read rate to rapid	X		X				X				X			
Disable interrupts		X		X		X		X		X		X		X
Enable interrupts	X		X				X				X			

REFERENCES

1. "Decision Table Programming and Reliability," *Proceedings of the Second International Conference on Software Engineering, 1976;* Lew and Tamanaha.

Advocates the use of decision tables for general computing applications. Shows examples drawn from several application areas.

2. "Translation of Decision Tables," *ACM Computing Surveys,* June, 1974; Pooch.

Contrasts decision tables with flowcharts, showing advantages and disadvantages. Discusses structure, types, and notation of decision tables, and their applicability to various types of problems. Automated translation techniques are then described.

3. RADC-TR-74-300, Structured Programming Series, Vol. 8 (Program Design Study), pp. 3-4 through 3-9, 1974.

Discusses the decision table: its use, layout, and advantages and disadvantages.

3.2.3.3 PROGRAM DESIGN LANGUAGES

Several trends in the software world have led to the evolution of a relatively recent concept, the program design language.

A *program design language* (PDL) is a nongraphic software design representation using a stylized, design-oriented language. The language should facilitate the representation of structure and control of a computer program.

For example, the reading of this book could be represented in a program design language as

```
Open book;
While page not back cover:
    Read page;
    Turn page if odd-numbered
End While
Close book;
```

The example illustrates the impact of the recent trends on the origin of the PDL. Note that in addition to the more obvious differences with respect to a flowchart, the directional arrows present in the flowchart are missing, and indentation has been used to group common actions dependent on a higher level of control. This may suggest to the alert reader the impact of structured programming methodology, which stresses sequential control constructs augmented by certain predefined conditionals and loops (such as While), and the elimination of the GOTO, which is often represented in a flowchart by a forward- or backward-pointing arrow. One of the trends that has acted as a forcing function on the development of PDLs, then, has been structured programming, which found the flowchart to be a relatively incompatible tool.

Another trend evolves from the inherent problems that accompany the flowcharting process itself. The original drawing of the flowchart, for example, requires at least a mild degree of graphic arts skills; the drawing of flowcharts by programmers, especially for documentation and even design, is at best an annoying task. Worse yet, the correction/update of a flowchart is nontrivial. The original graphic art process must be repeated for each update, often in its entirety. Splicing in a correction simply does not work.

The PDL is compatible with both of these trends. PDL can easily be used to represent a structured program; no graphics are used in the creation of a PDL representation; and updating a PDL representation is as simple as updating program source code (it can be done using a text editor, for example).

So far in this discussion, the emphasis has been on contrasting the PDL with the flowchart. The PDL tool is a valid concept in its own right, however. The designer using a PDL is much closer to the representation level that will eventually be used by the implementor, for example; if the PDL is syntactically consistent with the intended programming language, it may actually evolve directly into the code. And if a formally defined PDL is used, a computer-aided consistency check of the design becomes feasible (a consistency checker might spot unused data items or unreachable logic, for example). At the very least, PDL could be embedded in the implementation code as commentary, to enhance design-implementation traceability. Many doors are opened, or at least moved ajar, by the notion of a non-graphics-oriented design representation.

Some controversy has arisen around the degree of formality that should be used in specifying a PDL. Advocates of formality cite rigor and automated consistency checks as advantages of their point of view; opponents cite the constraints of formality on the mental process of design ("using this methodology slows down and warps my thought processes"), and the lack of knowledge inherent in the state of the art. As a result, PDLs vary from extremely well defined, formally specified languages, to "pidgin English."

State of the Art in Program Design Language

The inertia factor has tended to inhibit the use of PDLs; as a result, they are not heavily used in practice. In addition, although the concept of a PDL is well understood, there are few well-defined PDLs to choose from, and thus the designer wishing to use a PDL may need to define his own.

Cost of Program Design Language

The PDL is less expensive, in general, than commonly accepted alternatives. The difference in cost ranges from trivial, if the realm of consideration is that of design aid, to mildly significant, if the realm is that of formal and publishable design representation. As formality is introduced, the cost of usage may increase, although this is unclear; however, use of an automated consistency checker will, of course, entail substantial acquisition costs, depending on availability. (For the benefits of such a design checker, see Section 3.2.4.)

Example of Program Design Language

You have once again been assigned to elaborate the book reading design:

```
Open book to page 1;
Set reading pace to thorough;
Disable interrupts;
While page not back cover:
    Start reading page;
    If page interesting
    then
        If there is an interrupt and interrupts are enabled;
            then
                exit while-page-not-back-cover loop;
```

```
            else
                Finish reading page;
            end if
        else daydream; set reading pace to rapid; enable interrupts; end else
        end if
        Set page to next;
        Turn page if odd-numbered;
    End while page not back cover
    Close book;
```

Note that although this design is not graphic, the indentation of various levels of conditionality lends a graphic flavor to it. Note also the program code flavor of the representation.

REFERENCES

1. RADC-TR-74-300, Structured Programming Series, Vol. 8 (Program Design Study), pp. 4-1 through 5-5, 1974.

Advocates the PDL as an adjunct to structured programming. Describes PDLs, including "pseudo code," "playscript," and "pidgin English" forms. Discusses advantages and disadvantages. Shows examples of problems represented in PDL.

2. "PDL—A Tool for Software Design," *Proceedings of the National Computer Conference, 1975;* Caine and Gordon.

Describes a somewhat formalized PDL based on pidgin English. Shows examples of problems and discusses possible future directions in PDLs.

3.2.3.4   HIERARCHIC INPUT-PROCESS-OUTPUT

Hierarchic input–process–output (HIPO) is a graphic technique used to show function and data flow at the system overview level.

One common problem with representations of all kinds, whether the representation shows the interrelationships of human beings or the design of a piece of software, is the difficulty of showing both function and communication. Other design representation techniques discussed in this chapter tend to show function but not data flow. HIPO makes provision for both.

HIPO does not, however, attempt to break down the functions to be performed into detailed organizational and logical components.

For this reason it is more applicable, as a design representation, to a system overview than to a detail design. As pointed out in the reference, HIPO has, however, been used for detail representation as well. It is also useful for representing system requirements in a graphical manner.

A HIPO representation of the reading of a book could be as follows:

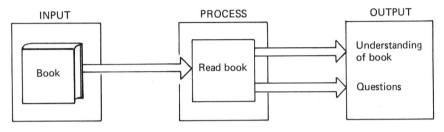

Figure 3.5

State of the Art in HIPO

HIPO is a relatively new concept. It is generally packaged with the structured programming groups of tools, and as a result it is used most in computing shops employing that technology. Although it is applicable outside that environment, it is not commonly used elsewhere.

Cost of HIPO

The cost of HIPO is not significantly more than alternative techniques. The only cost involved, as with other design representation schemata, is the cost of learning how to do it. Because HIPO is a graphic technique, drawing of the representation may require special skills, but the added cost should be trivial.

Example of HIPO

Once more, you have been asked to elaborate the book reading design as shown in Fig. 3.6.

Note that no attempt has been made to order the processing activities.

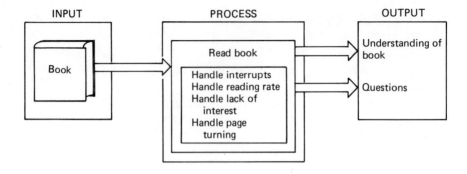

Figure 3.6

REFERENCES

1. "HIPO and Integrated Program Design," *IBM Systems Journal,* Vol. 15, No. 2, 1976; Stay.

Relates HIPO charts to the top-down (structured) design process, showing examples of their use in data processing applications.

2. RADC-TR-74-300, Structured Programming Series, Vol. 8 (Program Design Study), pp. 6-1 through 6-11, 1974.

Discusses the HIPO technique, showing several examples. Describes the purpose of HIPO and experience using it.

3.2.4   Automated design checking

Feedback mechanisms are the essence of reliability technology. It is one thing to do a design and formulate a representation; it is another to know that the design you have created has a chance of being correct. Design reviews, of course, are one form of feedback. Another is the automated design checker.

An automated design checker is a computer program that accepts a design representation as input, analyzes that design, and prints out a list of flaws in, and other descriptive information about, the design.

A couple of things are immediately obvious—the design representation must be computer-readable; and the analysis performed cannot progress much beyond an analysis of the form and structure (syntax?) of the design, as opposed to its content (semantics?). A typical automated design checker, for example, might detect inability to terminate a process (if it is blatant), unreachable functions, functions with no successor functions, and inconsistent interfunction connections. The design checker can produce additional usable outputs, such as a cross-reference list of data items referenced, and the design's procedure call structure. In addition, it can audit the design for conformance to design standards.

Regarding the computer readability of the design representation, the automated design checker must demand both a representation that is at least capable of being input nongraphically (although future changes in the state of the art could remove this requirement), and a relatively formal representation so that design elements with different meanings can be distinguished. Formality of design representation is a controversial topic—there are those who feel the use of formality increases rigor, and there are others who find it constraining—and the automated design checker concept is thus thrust into an arena in which its presence is at best uncomfortable.

State of the Art in Automated Design Checking

The concept of automated design checking is less than a half-dozen years old. For this reason, and because of the computer-readable and formality problems previously mentioned, it is so far little used. Some computing shops which have standardized on a relatively formal and readable design representation, however, have built design checkers and require their use. A few checkers of relatively general applicability are now available in the software marketplace.

Cost of Automated Design Checking

The acquisition cost of an automated design checker, unless one can be purchased off the shelf, will be at least moderate—perhaps $50,000 at professional salaries and industrial overheads.

Usage cost is relatively minor; if no design errors are found, the cost is trivial; and if some *are* found, the cost has been more than paid by the result.

Example of Automated Design Checking

You are still worried, even after a good design review, about the design of your elephant simulation program. You have represented the design in a relatively formal program design language (it has a predefined list of allowable verbs, and each line of PDL must begin with one of them). As a result, since the PDL is computer-readable and the formality makes it computer-decipherable, you decide to use a fortuitously available automated design checker.

You have the PDL keypunched in a form acceptable to the program. Submitting the PDL and appropriate job control input, you await the results.

The checker output is largely positive. It catches a few improperly nested if-thens, notes several PDL statements that failed to begin with an acceptable verb, and locates a program segment that cannot be logically reached. (The trunk simulation was still misplaced.) In addition, an inspection of the data item cross-reference listing shows several items referenced but not set, and one set but never referenced.

Correcting these errors does not give you total confidence, of course. You are glad to eliminate those errors, but you are realistic enough to know that semantic errors may remain in your design. However, you do feel confident that the types of errors checked for are now removed from your design.

REFERENCES

1. "Some Experience with Automated Aids to the Design of Large Scale Reliable Software," *Proceedings of the International Conference on Reliable Software, 1975;* Boehm, McClean, and Urfrig.

Summarizes experience in analyzing and eliminating design error sources. Describes a prototype automated system (DACC, design assertion consistency checker) used on a large-scale software project. Stresses differences between small and large projects. Categorizes design error causes.

2. "Software Design Validation Tool," *Proceedings of the International Conference on Reliable Software, 1975;* Carpenter and Tripp.

Describes DECA (design expression and confirmation aid), an automated design checker, which uses design trees and transition diagrams as input. Input design representations are described, and the DECA implementation is presented in overview. User experience is discussed ("it is highly cost effective").

3.   "PDL—Program Design Language Reference Guide," 1977; Caine, Farber, and Gordon.

User manual for a commercially available design checker. Shows example input and output, including data item cross-reference lists and procedure call structure.

3.3   IMPLEMENTATION TECHNIQUES

The fabrication of software is the center of a number of fascinating controversies. Controversy number one, mentioned in an earlier paragraph, is the issue of whether software is or should be fashioned by software craftsmen or by an assembly-line (less skilled) process. Historically, software development has been a cottage industry, most people would agree; but what of the future? Do we know enough to automate its production, using relatively unskilled coders; or is the product of the programmer's trade complex enough that we cannot (or perhaps should not) standardize the process?

Controversy number two is the issue of new methodologies. Structured programming and its periphery of new technology has taken the industry by storm. Is it indeed possible to write error-free software? Advocates of structured programming says that it is, that they have done it. Others scoff at such claims, saying that it rarely has happened and disputing even the specific claims of the SP advocates.

These two controversies are intertwined. Implicit in structured programming methodology is the belief that there is one "best" way to program, a way that everyone should use, a way that in fact should be imposed by standards. That way stresses the simple, straightforward approach to problem solution. It is a way that could conceivably move from standardization to regularization, and from regularization to assembly lining. Some advocates of SP, knowing that software managers lust after a future characterized by programmers screwing modules onto a top-down software structure moving down an assembly line, seldom bother to dim that vision.

At the same time, SP brings with it a fascinating bag of new tools which the software craftsman has desperately needed to beef up his historic cottage industry workbench. Thus SP has already helped the craftsman, but may lead to his demise!

But enough of philosophizing. There are very real problems in maintaining software reliability during the implementation process, and very real solutions.

The material that follows discusses some of those techniques. It may be interesting, however, to read this material at two levels—one, taking the material at face value, and the other, playing it against the controversies that swirl around the concepts.

3.3.1 Top-down versus bottom-up programming

Top-down programming is the practice of implementing and testing software in hierarchic sequence, starting first with those modules closest to the requirements for the software product.

Bottom-up programming is the practice of implementing and testing software in a reverse hierarchic sequence, starting first with the lowest-level modules, those farthest from the requirements.

Advocates of top-down stress that their approach is more natural, gives better management visibility, and eliminates the often-painful software integration process where bottom-up developed modules must be glued together.

Advocates of bottom-up stress that their approach leads to more solidly tested software modules, better definition and use of shared, common modules, and is easier to staff with programmers.

To understand top-down and bottom-up programming, a program should be viewed as a tree structure or network of modules, with the top level of the structure containing the control elements as defined by the requirements. Typically, the structure widens downward from the top, as the control module invokes subordinate functions, each of which invokes others.

A top-down implementation is one in which the highest level is coded first; the next level is then coded and integrated via testing into the program; and similarly until the bottom of the structure is reached. Each uncoded module is represented in the integrated whole by a stub code, which satisfies the interface requirements of the missing module but performs few or none of its functions. Stubs are replaced by, or augmented to become, the real thing when appropriate in the implementation plan. At any point in the implementation process, the implemented program should be correctly functioning down to the level of its current completeness.

Bottom-up programming, on the other hand, is implementation beginning at the lowest-level modules. It is typically tested via the concept of test drivers, starting with "unit testing" of the lowest levels and concluding with "integration testing" of the fully combined units.

It is the elimination of the separate integration phase of software development that makes top-down attractive from a reliability viewpoint. Since each piece of program is tested as it is screwed into the whole, when the program has been completely implemented, it has also been completely tested. Integration is incrementally accomplished rather than occurring as an indigestible whole. Errors and misunderstandings are identified and corrected early in the implementation.

Bottom-up uses testing techniques of known feasibility. Top-down, being newer, is less well understood. Bottom-up eliminates risk; top-down may reduce cost and increase reliability.

Both require their users to exercise special care—with bottom-up, keeping overall project goals in mind; with top-down, gaining a good understanding of the operating environment before coding. Failure in either case may lead to serious redesign during implementation.

State of the Art in Top-Down
and Bottom-Up Programming

Bottom-up programming is a common and accepted practice. Top-down is relatively new—it was first mentioned in the literature about 10 years ago, when it was referred to as "incremental implementation," but it received little attention until the advent of structured programming methodology. It remains little used in practice; this is largely because of its newness, not because of any known flaws in the concept. It *is* true, however, that the top-down approach requires both a new managerial and technological emphasis, and thus is inhibited by inertia more than some of the other aspects of structured programming.

A compromise between the two may actually resolve this dichotomy. Top-down is most attractive for its elimination of integration; bottom-up is most attractive for its use of common, well-checked-out building blocks. It may well be possible to do both. Using the "top-down/bottom-up" approach, initial software development would first implement the overall logic framework, then the lowest-level and most commonly used building blocks, and then proceed via the top-down approach. Levels of implementation and checkout would proceed downward from the top, but building blocks would be added as the need arose. This compromise could result in the best of both technologies.

Cost of Top-Down and Bottom-Up Programming

The relative costs of top-down and bottom-up are unclear. The only known cost difference would be training costs for those not already familiar with the newer top-down methodology. In the long run, the cost reductions achievable by the elimination of a separate integration phase may result in top-down being the more economical technique.

Example of Top-Down and Bottom-Up Programming

You are now at the point of implementing the baseball-playing simulation program which you specified in an earlier section. (It will be used for training baseball managers, you may remember.) You wonder about the relative wisdom of the top-down and bottom-up methodologies. Your design, emerging from the specification, has been performed in top-down fashion.

After some research, you elect to use a top-down/bottom-up compromise approach. This will track well with the elements of your top-down design, and you like the notion of eliminating the integration phase and of having a demonstrable product early in the implementation process (it will impress your manager and your customer, and may even ward off a project abort if times get tough, you know). Your implementation will proceed in top-down manner, but there are some bottom-level building blocks you will immediately need. For one, you need a random-number generator able to incorporate statistics-based factors specific to individual simulated players; for another, you need a data base management scheme for keeping and updating statistics and for such mundane things as base contents management.

However, with these building blocks designed, implemented, and tested, you are able to proceed in a top-down manner. You have already determined, in your design, that the top level of abstraction—simulation of a game of baseball—is immediately followed by a next lower level, consisting of a player roster manipulator, a play-by-play simulator, and a report generator. You begin work on the play-by-play simulator, stubbing off for the moment the roster manipulation and report generation. You implement the basic framework of play-by-play actions, coding stubs for specific actions (e.g., what to do if a left-handed batter faces a right-handed pitcher). You then go to work on the roster manipulation, replacing the stubs with high-level mechanisms for initiating and updating roster information. However, you stub off the lineup selection process as being too detailed for this level. It is now obvious that in order to see whether your simplistic simulator is functioning properly, you must have at least rudimentary report generation capability. You implement the inning-by-inning summary point but stub off the statistics and final summary modules.

Now that your simulator is running and printing results, you can go to work on the deeper details. The routine that distinguishes between hits and outs is coded, but the code for specific kinds of hits (singles, home runs, . . .) is deferred. Lineup selection is added to roster management, but use of individual player statistics is deferred. Report generation is expanded to printing opening lineups and names of batters. You are proceeding level by level, implementing and testing new capabilities one at a time, at each level producing a working program version with somewhat more in-depth capability than the previous version.

Your customer is especially pleased. Whenever he drops by, he can see that you have a functioning program, one that prints baseball-like results. Progress is discernible and measurable. You have come to like the top-down (albeit bottom-up!) approach.

REFERENCES

1.   "Software Design and Structuring," *Practical Strategies for Developing Large Software Systems,* Addison-Wesley, 1975; Boehm.

Discusses error sources ("design accounts for 64%, coding 36%") and timing of their discovery ("54% are found during or after acceptance test, and most are design errors"). Defines top-down and bottom-up approaches, their advantages/disadvantages, as well as several other approaches to more reliable software.

2. "Structured Programming in a Production Programming Environment," *Proceedings of the IEEE International Conference on Reliable Software, 1975;* Baker.

Discusses structured programming (SP) and its history at IBM Federal Systems Division. Gives guidelines for "top-down development" as well as the other elements of SP. Calls top-down "the most difficult of the four components (of SP) to introduce, probably because it requires the heaviest involvement and changes of approach on the part of programming managers," but goes on to say that it also has the greatest effect on reliability.

3. "Testing Principles," *Software Reliability,* Wiley–Interscience, 1976; Myers.

Contrasts top-down and bottom-up testing techniques; suggests a middle ground called "sandwich testing" which preserves the best of both. Evaluates the various methods.

4. "Top Down Programming in Large Systems," *Debugging Techniques in Large Systems,* Prentice-Hall, 1971; Mills.

Describes and advocates top-down programming. Stresses structured programming and its top-down implementation.

3.3.2 Modular programming

Modular programming is the practice of implementing software in small, functionally oriented pieces. These pieces are called *modules* and are usually implemented as subroutines or functions or clusters of subfunctions. (In some languages, "paragraphs" or "procedures" may be used.) Each module is devoted to one or more tasks related to a function; the module may be accessed from one or several places in a software system.

By isolating functions into separate code units, several advantages are gained—the software is more easily designed, built, comprehended, tested, and modified, since the structure is easily related to the tasks being performed. Additionally, the concept of a library of software procedures is made possible; pluggable modules may be built and used in a large number of different software systems. The latter is an especially powerful reliability concept, since a library typically contains oft-tested, highly stable code (such as a Fortran math and I/O library).

In most traditional programming languages, a module is considered to be a separately compiled or "external" subprogram. With more modern block structured languages, it is also possible to define modules as "internal" subprograms.

Superimposed over these discussions of structure must be a discussion of data communication. Most commonly data are passed to and from modules by parameter lists. Data are also passed by means of globally known data, or common blocks (Fortran) or compools (JOVIAL). The term *completely closed* is sometimes used to describe a module whose data are passed only through parameter lists. Such modules can have no "side effects" on common data base items and are transportable to other tasks or projects without carrying along a data base. Because of this, they are a preferred form of module.

However, the data needs of a module, especially in a complex program, are sometimes sufficiently diverse that a global or common/compool data base must be used instead of, or in addition to, a parameter list. These may be called *partially closed* modules. Internal procedures often utilize this form of data communication because the data base is readily and inexpensively accessible without the sometimes tedious manipulation of external data blocks.

An emerging concept is that of the *cluster,* which consists of a global data base associated with one or more procedures or subroutines that access it. Limitations are placed on accessing the data from outside the cluster. Thus the need for globally accessible data is effectively merged with the need for data base reliability.

A word of warning should be made about the readability of modular code. Because closed modules are usually off-page references—that is, the executable code is not present in the program listing at the point of invocation—it is at first reading difficult to follow a modular program. However, once the module functions are understood, code reading is improved by modular programming.

There is some conflict between modular programming and some interpretations of structured programming. Top-down design, an SP concept, often is defined as being the process of defining the structure of a program downward from its requirements, with each "branch" of the program's tree structure being self-contained. The notion of a tree structure, if taken literally (as it has been by some authors), implies no cross-communication among branches. This is at odds with the multiple-use subfunction concept, where one module may be accessed from several branches of the tree. Thus modular programming, and the development of project-independent libraries of common subfunctions, is incompatible with this project-driven interpretation of top-down design. Fortunately, few software-knowledgeable people advocate this interpretation.

State of the Art in Modular Programming

Modular programming has been acknowledged as a viable and useful concept in all but the earliest years of computing, when it was unknown. There is still little doubt that its many advantages, of which the reliability aspects are only a part, make it unquestionably a technique to be used on all software development tasks.

Cost of Modular Programming

Modular programming is as inexpensive as any viable alternative. It does require the use of linkage loaders which have the capability of accessing libraries of common modules, but this technology has been with us for so long that it can usually be taken for granted.

Example of Modular Programming

You have already begun a functional, building-block breakdown of your baseball simulation program in the preceding section. Remember that it consisted of a couple of bottom-up entities—a random-number generator and a data base manager—and then a host of top-down entities. Each of those entities will now become a module of code.

As you proceed further in defining functional modules, the top-down/bottom-up implementation proceeds. The player roster manipulator, the play-by-play simulator, and the report generator become modules each containing many calls to tasks performed by them for other modules. The play-by-play, for example, delegates several of its functions as follows: There is a base-path manager module, which keeps track of the answer to Abbott/Costello questions about "Who's on First"; there is a play-by-play decision-maker module, which mixes the individual player statistics and the random-number results to come up with the result of each batter's action; and there is a statistics update module, which accesses the data base to record the results of the play-by-play decision maker. Modules correspond to the elements in the top-down design and to the building blocks of the implementation "tree structure." Each module with elements "below" it in the tree invokes those elements in a modular fashion, usually by a procedure call.

You find your implementation process to be one of "thinking modular"—when a function appears to be needed more than once, or subject to change, or sufficiently complex to clutter up main-line logic, you modularize it. The resulting program, you know from experience, will be relatively easy to change when the inevitable requirements changes start coming in.

REFERENCES

1. *Reliable Software Through Composite Design,* Petrocelli/Charter, 1975; Myers.

Advocates modularity, if done properly, as the key to effective software development. Describes proper modularizing—how to design them, how to interrelate them. Stresses the importance of the design phase.

2. "The Influence of Software Structure on Reliability," *Proceedings of IEEE International Conference on Reliable Software, 1975;* Parnas.

Distinguishes between reliability (delivering usable services) and correctness (meeting specifications). Emphasizes the importance of the former and stresses modularizing to promote it. Poses questions pertinent to module definition.

3. "On the Criteria to Be Used in Decomposing Systems into Modules," *Communications of the ACM,* Dec., 1972; Parnas.

Uses an example to discuss two strategies for defining modules. Recommends modularizing to promote "information hiding," such that modules contain design decisions that are likely to change.

4. "Notes on the Design of Euclid," *Proceedings of an ACM Conference on Language Design for Reliable Software, 1977;* Popek, Horning, Lampson, Mitchell, and London.

Describes a language for writing system programs, called Euclid, which stresses capabilities for verification. Contains a good discussion on the Euclid philosophy of module/cluster definition.

3.3.3 Fault-tolerant software

Most of the efforts toward making software more reliable are devoted to methodology leading toward the elimination of errors. *Fault tolerance,* on the other hand, explores ways of making software that *has* errors continue to function successfully in spite of them.

That task is harder than the words used to describe it may make it sound. How do you anticipate, for example, an error, when if you knew it existed you would obviously seek to eliminate it? And, since software errors are almost always repeatable, once an operational piece of software is discovered to be in error, how does a software system adjust itself to overcome the problem?

The problem is thus rather different from computer hardware fault tolerance, which is a tempting source of analogy. Software, unlike hardware, does not wear out from heavy usage, nor does it drop bits and later perform satisfactorily. Software fault tolerance thus must seek its own solutions to its own unique problems.

The essence of software fault tolerance methodologies to date seems to boil down to the following techniques:

1. *Error confinement.* Program in such a way that errors do not contaminate portions of the program beyond that which created them.
2. *Error detection.* Program tests for and reactions to errors when they arise.
3. *Error recovery.* Program procedures for resuming correct processing after an error.
4. *Dual programming.* Program redundant backup code which can substitute at least momentarily for faulty code.

Just as fault tolerance is easier said than done, so are these techniques more complicated than they sound. How do you confine errors? How do you switch from faulty code to good code? How do you recover without crashing totally? Answers to those questions are consuming the efforts of a number of researchers.

A few tentative answers can be given now, however. Errors can be confined by utilizing a concept sometimes called the *principle of least privilege.* Procedures and data should have limited and well-defined functions such that no procedure offers more capabilities than are needed for its intended function and no procedure can access data outside of its own limited-access data base. Errors can be detected via extra code explicitly testing key variables for correctness. Recovery can be achieved with extra code which replaces bad data with good, and bad code with backup good code. And dual programming can be used to achieve backup code.

The latter notion is especially intriguing. Software errors, as previously mentioned, tend to be repeatable. It would do no good to unplug a piece of faulty software and replace it with an identical but not "wornout" copy, since software does not wear out. Thus backup code must be the same as, but different from, the mainline code.

Dual programming is the practice of implementing software twice by two independent teams. The result of dual programming is two different code implementations which satisfy the same set of requirements. Given the typical complexity of software, it is extremely unlikely that both implementations will fail on any given task.

There are some reliability fringe benefits to dual programming. Each team may do a better job, owing to the competition factor, and checking results of testing may be easier since each implementation may be treated as a "hand calculation" for the other.

State of the Art in Fault-Tolerant Software

Fault tolerance is still largely a concern of the research world, but that situation may change rapidly. Real-time systems sometimes have critical needs to stay on the air no matter what happens. A digital flight control system for a 747, for example, cannot afford to abort and throw up its symbolic hands with the lives of over 300 people at stake. Even the operating system on your friendly local computer system should (but perhaps doesn't) have the capability to be crash-proof, especially if it supports on-line users. Thus, in the critical software world, fault tolerance is beginning to become an accepted but still new evolutionary methodology.

Dual programming, however, is not yet commonly used. One advocate says that most technologists view it as an "April Fool's joke." After years of emphasis on reducing software costs and increasing productivity, the idea of doing a job twice boggles the mind!

Cost of Fault-Tolerant Software

The production of fault-tolerant software will cost more, perhaps considerably more. The cost of producing backup code by dual programming alone, for example, may nearly double development costs. Dual programming requires not just dual coding, but also dual design and dual testing using two different teams of programmers. (Having the same team do the job twice, or starting both implementations from the same design, won't work since a given "mindset" will probably result in consistent errors.)

Error confinement, detection, and recovery incur additional costs. One expert in fault-tolerant software sees total costs increasing by at least 35%. At this point in the evolution of fault-tolerant software, that estimate may be optimistic.

Example of Fault-Tolerant Software

You have just learned that your baseball-playing simulator will be delivered to the despotic leader of a remote nation and that you personally will be invited to perform the installation. You are warned by your management, in a friendly gesture, that the despot takes unkindly to faulty technology and has been known to remove the coding fingers of programmers whose work is below par.

Because you now perceive your application to be what is called "critical software," you decide to employ all possible software reliability techniques. As a "safety play," in case all else fails, you use fault-tolerant technology. You perform a new analysis of your baseball simulator, studying the modularization concepts with new criteria in mind. Fortunately, your modules were selected and implemented using the principle of "information hiding," and you decide that they effectively confine errors as well. However, you design a new error detection and recovery mechanism: anomalous conditions are to be tested for at every stage of the program's execution. The result, you realize, is a rigorous blanket of assertions and assertion checks manually and permanently inserted in the program (see also Section 3.4.2.3). Detected assertion violations are processed by a central recovery module, which mixes specific assertion violation responses with a general recovery mechanism designed to keep the program properly executing. For example, if the value of variable "outs" is ever (inappropriately) more than 3, the program, having detected the condition, branches to the "next inning" label, meanwhile logging the assertion violation on a system tape for later review.

You also define the areas where backup code is necessary and the mechanisms for control transfer from mainline to backup. Most of these are situation-specific: the entire base-path manager, for example, is backed up so that if, for example, a violation occurs on the assertion that each base can be occupied by no more than one player, the program (after logging the violation) can backtrack to the preceding play and repeat its impact with the newly-switched-in backup code. You then select your most skilled peer to write the backup code, and, without explaining all the details to him, you invite him to participate in the delivery and installation.

He accepts. You decide to fill him in on the political details later.

REFERENCES

ACM Computing Surveys, Dec., 1976, is a special issue on fault-tolerant software. It contains these articles:

1.   "Fault-Tolerant Operating Systems"; Denning.

Stresses error confinement, and defines error confinement principles. Uses operating system methodology to illustrate the concepts. Discusses principles that should be used in operating system design and implementation.

2.   "Fault-Tolerant Software for Real-Time Applications"; Hecht.

Cites the need for software fault-tolerance methodologies in the real-time environment, to match hardware fault tolerance. Stresses detection, recovery, and backup techniques. Shows examples in skeleton routines. Economics are discussed.

3.   "Operating System Structures to Support Security and Reliable Software"; Linden.

Focuses on security and its reliability implications, and the use of error confinement by small protection domains and extended-type objects (entities with a unique set of operations that can be performed on them). Access control on these objects is stressed. "The ideas discussed . . . involve a substantial amount of discontinuity with the past."

3.3.4   Other coding concepts

There are many other "good coding practices" whose chief value is to improve productivity or maintainability of code but which have peripheral benefit on software reliability. Chief among these are the use of a high-order language, structured coding, and programming standards.

High-order languages (HOLs) have enormous benefit in the majority of software applications areas, largely in software productivity. Reliability benefits accrue for the same reasons that productivity benefits accrue—the programmer who codes in HOL codes many fewer statements than the assembly language programmer and thus has many fewer chances for error. In addition, the HOL programmer is screened from a whole class of error potential situations related to hardware intimacy. The compiler, not the programmer, is responsible for selecting specific machine instructions and registers and making all the other hardware-dependent choices. The HOL programmer can concentrate on the application he is solving rather than the hardware on which the solution will run. For that reason HOLs have also been called "problem-oriented languages."

Structured coding is the coding of software solutions where the emphasis is placed on straightforward logical structures. It is an element of the "structured programming" methodology mentioned frequently in other sections of this guidebook. Structured coding would limit control structures to a sequence of two operations; a conditional branch to one of two operations (IF-THEN-ELSE); return repetition of an operation (DO-WHILE and DO-UNTIL); and multibranch selection between operations (CASE). By implication, the direct branch (GOTO) is eliminated. The reliability benefits of structured coding center on the simplified logic structure; a simpler program is easier to code, easier to understand, and easier to modify. Errors resulting from logical complexity are thus minimized.

Programming standards are the requirements placed on a programmer by his environmental control structure. They may be dictated by his management, or by his customer, or perhaps even by his peers. They are over and above, however, the requirements of his application or his language or his compiler or his computer. They are imposed to improve productivity and readability and perhaps portability. Reliability benefits of programming standards emerge from the other benefits; readable software, for example, is considerably safer to modify without introducing errors. Typical standards might include naming conventions (e.g., "all variables in data structure RECORD1 must begin with RECORD1"); limits on code complexity (e.g., "subprograms cannot contain more than 60 lines of code"); limits of programming construct usage (e.g., "GOTOs must not be used"). Code auditors, discussed in the section on structural analysis, are a tool for verifying adherence to programming standards. Since programming standards vary considerably depending on local beliefs and needs, it is difficult to generalize about their value in software reliability.

The coding concepts above are not dealt with in depth here, for a variety of reasons.

The benefits of a high-order language are well known and covered elsewhere; it needs only to be said here that the reliability benefits of HOL code are roughly commensurate with the productivity benefits, and thus are significant.

Structured coding's reliability benefits are less obvious and less significant; in addition, the use or lack of use of structured coding is usually dependent on such installation-dependent factors as language standards, since most contemporary languages cannot be used for structured coding without enhancement. For example, Fortran before Fortran 77 had almost no structured coding constructs and could only be used for structured coding via awkward support concepts such as precompilers. A *precompiler* is a translator that converts a specialized language (e.g., Fortran enhanced with IF-THEN-ELSE and DO-WHILE) to a standard language (e.g., Fortran). The problem with a precompiler is that not only does it remove its user one more level from his operational program, but he must function at all those levels. That is, he needs the memory map and cross-reference list from the standard language compiler, for example, and his debug output at the object code level from the operating system. Correlating all that with his original program listing can be somewhat traumatic. Thus structured coding techniques may enhance software reliability, but the use of a precompiler could well nullify that enhancement. A much preferable technique is to use a language that already has structured programming constructs, such as Algol or one of its derivatives, or a modern language such as Pascal or the Navy's SPL/I.

As mentioned before, programming standards reliability benefits are difficult to define specifically because of installation differences.

REFERENCES

1. "Languages and Structured Programs," *Current Trends in Programming Methodology,* Prentice-Hall, 1977; Wulf.

Discusses the "software crisis," the need for structure in programs, and the role of languages in providing it. Stresses newly emerging language concepts.

2. "Structured Programming in a Production Programming Environment," *Proceedings of the IEEE International Conference on Reliable Software, 1975;* Baker.

Discusses structured coding and programming standards in the context of the structured programming methodology.

3. "On the Development of Large Reliable Programs," *Current Trends in Programming Methodology,* Prentice-Hall, 1977; Linger and Mills.

Advocates structured programming as a tool for coding error-free programs; uses illustrative examples.

4. "Air Force Command and Control Information Processing in the 1980's; Trends in Software Technology," R-1012-PR, The Rand Corp., 1974; Kosy.

Describes the evolution and postulated future of software in command and control technology. Puts technological concepts into perspective, including HOL usage and benefits.

5. "Module Design and Coding," *Software Reliability,* Wiley–Interscience, 1976; Myers.

Stresses the importance of high-level language. Also discusses structured coding, standards, and other coding techniques.

6. "BCS Software Production Data," RADC-TR-77-116, 1977; Black, Curnow, Katz, and Gray.

Defines modern programming practices used at Boeing Computer Services. Contains as Section 2.0 an excellent discussion of traditional programming practices, against which structured/modern techniques are often compared.

3.4 CHECKOUT TECHNIQUES

The emphasis of the preceding sections has been on the "front-end loading" of software reliability activities. That is, errors that are squeezed out of the requirements and the design are that many fewer errors to come back and plague the programmer during his program testing process, and the user during operation.

It is tempting but naive to believe that this will totally rid a program of errors. The fact of the matter is, in these earlier phases no program even existed from which to remove bugs!

Checkout is the term that will be used in this guidebook for the phase of software development when the now-formed software product is (hopefully) cleansed of its flaws.

This section divides error-removal activities into two-classes—static methods, involving analysis of a program without executing it, and testing methods, involving execution of a program under test input conditions. Static methods generally involve high people-resource costs and low computer-resource costs; testing incurs high computer costs, and may involve high people costs as well. As will be seen, testing has traditionally been, and will continue to be, the largest focus of software reliability efforts. However, static methods have generated a great deal of enthusiasm in recent years, and may play an increasingly important role in the years to come.

REFERENCES

1. "Tutorial: Static Analysis and Dynamic Testing of Computer Software," *Computer (IEEE),* Apr., 1978; Fairley.

Defines static and dynamic methodologies. Describes techniques, pointing out both advantages and disadvantages/limitations.

2. "A Controlled Experiment in Program Testing and Code Walk-throughs/Inspections," Communications of the ACM, Sept., 1978; Myers.

Describes an experiment in error-seeking using testing and code review. Sees these techniques as complementary, with both being necessary.

3.4.1   Static methods

At this point in the software reliability effort, a piece of software actually exists. It exists in the form of a machine-readable representation, but, more important, it exists in human-readable form. The listing of a program, output by its compiling or assembling program, is that human-readable representation.

When most software people think of a computer program, they think of its listing. Fortunately, since the listing and the machine-readable representation are usually produced by the same processor, there is every reason to believe that each faithfully represents the other. The reason this is fortunate is that the listing serves as the basis for almost all understandings about a program, and, more specifically from the point of view of this section, it serves as the basis for most static reliability methodology. Reliability methodologies that do not involve examination of the listing usually involve an automated analysis of the source program itself. In either case, what distinguishes static methodologies from those in the next section (on testing) is that they do not involve execution of the program.

Specific static methodologies are described in the material that follows.

3.4.1.1 DESK CHECKING

Desk checking is probably computing's "oldest profession." Of all the elements of software development methodology, desk checking has been the most necessary for the longest time. Nothing is likely to change that situation (although, unlike other oldest professions, desk checking lacks stimulation and excitement and is sometimes avoided for those reasons).

It is a little difficult to define the concept. Desk checking is a term covering the totality of checkout efforts performed manually. Most commonly, it refers to (1) reviewing a program listing for faults, (2) doing arithmetic calculations to verify output value correctness and (3) "playing computer" (i.e., manually simulating program execution) in order to understand and verify program logic and data flow. What these three processes have in common is that they are performed at the desk rather than on the computer—hence the term.

One or more of the facets of desk checking described above is an essential part of any verification process. The choice among those facets is generally debug-driven—that is, desk checking efforts concentrate on areas of special problems, especially suspected errors or code inefficiencies, and involve techniques appropriate to that problem.

Arithmetic verification of output is especially essential. Although it is sometimes possible to do this by checking against already known correct answers, more often the only way to do it is by manual or calculator performance of the arithmetic chores of the program.

State of the Art in Desk Checking

As previously mentioned, desk checking is one of the earliest forms of software verification and continues to be a vital element of that process.

Part of the focus of modern software technology, however, has been to develop computer-assisted desk checking. "Let the computer do it" has become today's programmer cry, with good reason. Computer resources have grown increasingly cheap, and human resources increasingly dear, as the costs of computing evolve. Source language debug, interactive debug, and perhaps even symbolic execution are in some sense automated desk checking—they let the computer itself "play computer" while providing enough visibility for the programmer to monitor program flow.

However, there is really no significant substitute for manual at-the-desk checking, especially listing review and arithmetic calculation. Unfortunately, there is some evidence that the latter is becoming a neglected art. Manual arithmetic calculations are drudgery, and programmers would in general be happy to avoid them. Since there is no known effective substitute, this neglect may someday have tragic implications.

Cost of Desk Checking

Since desk checking is such an ill-defined concept, it is difficult to provide a cost estimate for its use. It is undoubtedly true, however, that moderate amounts of desk checking save more money than they cost.

Example of Desk Checking

Suppose that your program for the generation of probabilistic odds for bookmaking on games of chance has gone awry. The black-jack option is producing obviously erroneous results under test.

You suspend testing activities and begin an earnest and detailed review of the program listing. Statement by statement you proceed through the blackjack portion of the program, looking for flaws in the logic and the mathematics. But in spite of your dedicated efforts, no error manages to permeate your consciousness. (You have just employed desk checking of the listing analysis variety.)

Getting a little more concerned, you perform the probabilistic arithmetic as your mathematical algorithm specifies it, keeping track of all intermediate results in case you need to check them later against program-provided results. As you were fairly sure would be true, the hand-calculated results differ from those obtained by your program. Obviously, in spite of your listing review, there is an error somewhere in your coding of the algorithm. (You have just employed desk checking of the arithmetic calculation variety.)

You decide to play computer. Statement by statement, algorithmic term by algorithmic term, you read the program listing and perform the act dictated by the program. After each step, you check the results against the saved arithmetic results of the previous paragraph.

After several statements, you obtain a difference between the algorithmic hand-calculated results and your computer simulation hand-calculated results. Your brow indicates that an "ah-ha" reaction has occurred. The coded representation of the algorithm has used the wrong variable in a minor term of the probabilistic equation.

Having invested this much time in hand calculation, you decide to finish the playing computer approach to the algorithm, using the corrected equation, to see if any other errors remain. Fortunately, algorithmic and coded results track perfectly, and you now feel much more confident that the code is correct. (You have just employed desk checking of the playing computer variety.)

REFERENCES

1. Proverb 20, *Programming Proverbs for Fortran Programmers,* Hayden, 1975; Ledgard.

Advocates and describes "hand-checking your program before running it." Uses an example containing several hand-check-detectable errors.

A *peer code review* is a process by which a team of programming personnel do an in-depth review of a program or portion of a program, by inspection. Other terms used for this activity are code verification, code/program reading, and walk-through.

The primary reason for a peer code review is improving program reliability. The peer team examines the subject program intimately, from the various points of view of the various participants, seeking errors that may have eluded the programmer's less diverse frame of reference.

Peer reviews have some fringe benefits. Programmers are motivated to do a better job, knowing that their work will be critiqued by their peers. Additionally, programmers will collectively improve their techniques and style as they share concepts at the review, and reviewers will gain sufficient knowledge to serve in a backup capacity on the program if necessary.

However, there are also problems with peer reviews. Code review is often drudgery; the methodical pace necessary for effective review is supertaxing. Because of this motivation of participants is difficult. Motivation is vital, however, because only through intense reviewer concentration can the peer code review have value.

In addition, peer code reviews are expensive. Experience indicates that about 100 source statements may be reviewed in an hour, and the concentration of the participants wanes after an hour. For a program of any size, the cost and duration of a peer review may be prohibitive. Because of the value of the review, in such circumstances it might be wise to review key program portions and to select other portions for review randomly.

Several questions regarding the application of the peer code review need to be dealt with here.

Who Attends a Peer Code Review?

Only technologists should attend a peer review. Managers in general should be excluded, to avoid any emphasis on programmer review as opposed to program review. Typically three to four peers should attend, varying in experience level to maximize learning flow. Preferably, these participants should have some sense of responsibility for the program, such as being members of the same programming team, or having responsibility for an interfacing program, or being assigned to product testing or quality assurance, or to maintaining the program, or at the very least assuming backup responsibility as the result of review attendance.

Attitude is important among participants. Those who cannot be cooperative and tactful and nondefensive while striving for technical excellence should be excluded from peer code reviews (and perhaps from the organization).

When Should a Peer Code Review Be Held?

There is no clear answer to this question. There are those who suggest that they should occur as early as possible in the development cycle. However, it is recommended here that a peer code review should not occur until after coding of the program to be reviewed is complete, well annotated, and syntactically correct. Preferably, rudimentary semantic errors should also have been removed by early testing.

What Is the Sequence of Events at a Peer Code Review?

The methodology of a peer code review may best be worked out by the individual participants. Some, for example, may prefer to study the program listing prior to the review, or even conduct their portion of the review in isolation, providing written comments to the responsible programmer.

However, in general the responsible programmer will verbally lead the participants sequentially through the logic flow of the program as represented in the listing. All logic branches should be taken at least once. Someone should be assigned responsibility for recording significant comments. The function of each statement will be discussed as it is encountered. Program requirements and design specifications will be present for correlation of function to its driving factors.

State of the Art in Peer Code Review

Because peer code review is an essentially human endeavor, it is not a new concept in the overall software reliability scheme of things. However, historically the process has seldom been used except in times of particularly difficult error detection and removal. Thus it is fair to consider its regular application to the software development process as a "new" methodology, emerging at the time of the structured programming notion of chief programmer teams in the early 1970s.

Along with the other elements of structured programming, strong claims have been made for the value of the peer code review as a software reliability component. It may well be true that claims to have produced "error-free software," if valid, owe more to peer code review than to any other element of the structured programming milieu.

Cost of Peer Code Review

Peer code review is not cheap. Because of the number of participants involved and the intensity of the review process, consistent and complete use of the concept may add 10 to 50% to the cost of software implementation. Hopefully, improvements in reliability, attendant lowered maintenance costs, and cross-training benefits will more than compensate for this cost. However, since the latter tend to be difficult to measure (this is a bane of all reliability technology), it is unlikely that this trade-off can be quantified.

Example of Peer Code Review

You have completed your bookmaking program and it has occurred to you that it might prove personally useful. But since any such use would involve your own money rather than a customer's, you are determined to leave no reliability stone unturned in removing all potential errors in advance.

As a result, you hand-pick a few skilled friends, explain what you have in mind, and invite them to a peer code review in your recreation room.

In preparation for the review, you spread your program listing on a table, flanked by ample supplies of cheese, crackers, and chip dip. The requirements specifications, detailed design, and user manual are stacked conveniently on the floor, immediately next to a pitcher of beer and several icy bottles of Seven-Up. Arranging empty glasses strategically, you are ready for the arrival of your guests.

After a few convivial remarks, and a top-level program overview, you get down to business. Statement by statement, you explain the function of the program, stopping to field questions from reviewers and to wipe dip off the listing. The participants are positive in their approach, and a feeling of camaraderie permeates the group. As time progresses, however, the pace at which you move through the listing lessens noticeably, and some comments become more testy than constructive. Recognizing the symptoms, you bring the review to a close.

You hold a summary discussion. Everyone agrees that a great deal of progress has been made, and you have detected three programming errors and the need for improved self-documenting code (you could not remember, under questioning, the function of a couple of flag variables). The group parts amicably, and you put away the newly marked listing and the dead soldiers.

As a postscript, however, realizing that the 112 statements you managed to review was less than 10% of your program, you call your friends and invite them to the second in a proposed series of 10 code reviews.

No one shows up.

(Absurd as it may sound, this scenario actually happened.)

REFERENCES

1.   "Programming as a Social Activity," *The Psychology of Computer Programming,* Van Nostrand Reinhold, 1971; Weinberg.

Discusses "egoless programming" and individual ownership of programs. Advocates the team approach to software development and review. Uses an anecdotal approach.

2.   RADC-TR-74-300, Structured Programming Series, Vol. 15 (Validation and Verification Study), pp. 5-3 through 5-8, May, 1975.

Describes "code verification" and its methodology—how to read code, what to have available, who to involve, what to do, what to review, and what should result. Advantages and disadvantages are discussed.

3. "A Controlled Experiment in Program Testing and Code Walk-throughs/Inspections," Communications of the ACM, Sept., 1978; Myers.

Sees code review as a necessary but somewhat expensive component of the overall checkout process. Suggests the evolution of computer-assisted review techniques.

3.4.1.3 STRUCTURAL ANALYSIS

There is a class of software problems which could be unearthed by human-oriented static methodologies such as desk checking and peer code review if human beings were sufficiently patient. This class involves problems emerging from the structure—data structure and especially logic structure—of a program.

However, the elaborate efforts necessary to perform these kinds of analysis has led to the automation of the process. As a result, a variety of automated tools have been developed to explore a program looking for certain classes of structural problems. These tools fall into the "static" category because, even though they involve the use of an automated tool, the analysis is performed on the subject program without executing it.

A structural analyzer, then, is an automated tool that seeks and records errors in the structural makeup of a ("subject") computer program undergoing analysis. Examples of problems sought by structural analyzers include:

1. Data variables undeclared or improperly declared.
2. Data variables used before they are initialized, or initialized, and never used.
3. Use of unauthorized language forms (e.g., GOTO in structured programming, ALTER in COBOL, mixed-mode arithmetic).
4. Violation of naming conventions (data variables, subroutine names, statement labels).
5. Overly complicated constructs (loops or conditionals too deeply or improperly nested).

6. Subroutine argument checking (actual and formal parameter matching).
7. Inconsistencies in subroutine calling trees (inadvertent recursion).
8. Inconsistent global data layout (COMMON blocks).
9. Unreachable logic.
10. Missing logic.
11. Erroneous logic (potentially infinite loops).

Some of the errors above fall into the category of standards violations. That is, the technique used may be proper from the point of view of the language and compiler being used but not from the point of view of the installation or project needing the code. Structural analyzers that look specifically for such violations are commonly called *code auditors*. A code auditor might detect (using the preceding list) unauthorized language form usage, violation of naming conventions, and overly complicated constructs, for example.

Structural analyzers are almost always language-specific and, in the case of code auditors, installation- or project-specific. Most structural analyzers built to date accommodate only Fortran or COBOL. For example, DAVE, built at the University of Colorado, processes CDC 6000 Fortran programs looking for uninitialized variables via a very elaborate algorithm; and Meta COBOL, a COBOL preprocessor and auditor, looks for unauthorized language forms (ALTER, . . .), questionable constructs (deeply nested IFs, . . .), and other similar violations. On the other hand, software sneak analysis, for example, uses computer hardware concepts to look for software structure "short circuits" in assembler language code.

State of the Art in Structural Analysis

There is nothing new about the categories of errors sought by structural analyzers—those kinds of errors in general have been made by disgusted programmers since the first computers came into being.

The automated facet of structural analysis is, however, a relatively new concept, beginning in the early 1970s. Software tool builders have found structural analyzers a fertile area for exploration. As a result, there are a number of tools available. Few, however, are in common use. One of the references at the end of this section provides a good list of existing structural analyzers (categorizing them as "code auditors" and "static analyzers").

Cost of Structural Analysis

Acquisition of a structural analyzer is the major cost factor. Costs can range from trivial if the program is already in the public domain (Colorado has made DAVE available, and the U.S. government has a number of them) to upwards of $100,000 (at professional salaries and industrial overheads) for implementation of an elaborate analytical tool. A project-oriented code auditor, for example, might cost $20,000 to $40,000 to implement, depending on the difficulty of analysis of the specific standards employed.

Usage of a structural analyzer should not cause serious cost considerations. Neither computer time nor human results analysis time should be significant. Errors detected should more than pay for usage.

Example of Structural Analysis

Still determined to rid your bookmaking program of errors before you use it, you decide to subject it to a fortuitously available structural analyzer. You have coded the program in Fortran, and your installation procured a Fortran structural analyzer and code auditor a little over a year ago. (In fact, your decision to use Fortran was based partially on the existence of such tools.)

You submit a run to the computer consisting of the Job Control statements necessary to invoke the structural analyzer, and your bookmaking program source code. The analyzer is the kind that checks for referencing variables before they are initialized, inconsistence of logical structure, and conformance to installation standards.

When the results of the analysis come back, there is good news and bad news. The good news is that via the peer code review you scrubbed out all uninitialized variable and naming convention violations; no such error messages are printed out by the analyzer. The bad news is that a couple of your common blocks are inconsistent, one statement number is never referenced, and your statement numbers are occasionally out of order (that violates an installation standard).

The bad news is not very bad, however. The errors are easy to fix. Straightening out the common blocks is a near-clerical matter. Fixing the statement numbers is a little harder, since you need to detect and correct all references to them as well as correcting the numbers themselves. The statement number that is never referenced was supposed to have been, and you must add some code to do that. You do those things, make another run against the structural analyzer, and your program gets a clean bill of health.

At least as important as fixing the identified errors, you realize, is the knowledge that no errors of those classes tested for are likely to remain in your program.

REFERENCES

1. "Automated Tools for Software Quality Control," *Transactions of the Software '77 Conference;* Norum and Miller.

Defines and rationalizes the software quality control process as an evolving force in software development. Classifies and inventories available automated quality control tools, naming the tools and discussing their function and availability. Includes both static and dynamic tools.

2. "Some Experience with DAVE—A Fortran Program Analyzer," *Proceedings of the 1976 National Computer Conference;* Osterweil and Fosdick.

Discusses DAVE, an analyzer that examines multimodule ANSI Fortran programs for uninitialized variables, and variables initialized but unused. Describes its implementation and use.

3. "Software Sneak Analysis," *Proceedings of the AIAA Conference on Computers in Aerospace, 1977;* Godoy and Engels.

Describes a methodology based on hardware sneak-circuit-analysis techniques which involves converting a computer program into a hardware circuit representation, and analyzing the circuit for certain kinds of structural faults.

3.4.1.4   PROOF OF CORRECTNESS

Proof of correctness is the process of using mathematical theorem-proving concepts on a computer program or its design to show that it is consistent with its specification. This is done by breaking the program into logical segments, defining input and output assertions for each segment (an *input assertion* is a statement of what characteristics the input data to the segment must have; an *output assertion* is a similar statement about the output produced by the segment), and demonstrating that, when the program functions, if all input assertions are true then so, too, are all output assertions. It must also be shown that the program successfully terminates.

Showing termination is largely an ad hoc procedure. However, the correctness aspect is a well-defined procedure described as follows: The program is augmented with assertions as described above. The program is broken at the points where the assertions are attached, resulting in a set of program segments. For each program segment, the assertion at the bottom is passed backward through the program statements. The assertion is modified according to the semantics of the program statement through which it passed. The correctness of the segment is demonstrated by showing that the assertion which migrated to the top of the program segment follows from the assertion which was originally at the top.

There are many opinions on the value of program proof. Probably the most universally accepted opinion is that it is at least 10 years away from being useful on programs of any significance. In the context of this guidebook, where a menu of reliability tools is being presented for near-term project selection and use, proof of correctness has little value.

The advantages of proof of correctness are:

1. *Provides a rigorous, formalized process.*
2. *Forces analysis.* The proof of correctness process forces the programmer to consider sections of his program, which might otherwise only get a cursory analysis.
3. *Clarifies computation states.* Writing out the assertions makes the programmer explicitly state his heretofore implicit assumptions, which define the state of the computation for specific points within the program.
4. *Clarifies dependencies.* When executing the proof, the programmer becomes aware of what assumptions about the input data are implicitly used by the code in various sections of the system.

Disadvantages are:

1. *Complexity.* Even for small simple programs, the symbolic manipulations can be overly complex. This can lead to . . .
2. *Errors.* Because of the complexity it is easy to introduce errors into the computation of the statements to be proven as well as the proof of those statements.
3. *Arrays are difficult to handle.*
4. *Lack of powerful-enough theorem provers.* The proof process could be automated to reduce errors, except that there are no theorem provers powerful enough for most practical problems.
5. *Too much work.* It often requires several times the amount of work to prove a program than was required to write the program.
6. *Lack of expressive power.* It is often very difficult to create the output assertion for what is an intuitively simple computation.
7. *Nonintuitive.* The procedure tends to obscure the true nature of the computation being analyzed rather than providing insight into the computation.
8. *Requires training.* Like programming, the user of proof of correctness requires many hours of training as well as practice in order to use the technique well.

State of the Art in Proof of Correctness

Many researchers are currently working in the proof-of-correctness area. Small algorithms and programs have been proven in this environment. There has been little success in using the technique on problems of any significance.

Because of the feasibility questions regarding program proof, the concept of "informal proof of correctness" has been advocated. One approach to less-rigorous uses of these concepts is described in this guidebook under the title "assertion checker."

Cost of Proof of Correctness

Lack of practical experience with proof of correctness makes it difficult to quantify costs. Training costs, as mentioned before, are a consideration. Usage costs are nontrivial, perhaps adding 100 to 500% to the cost of the portion of the software being proven.

Example of Proof of Correctness

Carried onward by your earlier success in removing bugs from your bookmaking program, you elect to use proof of correctness techniques. In order to learn more about the technique, however, you decide to try it out on a much smaller problem first.

The problem you choose is the calculation of X^n, represented by the code that follows. The facts that you know to be true about the problem—the input assertions—are included as "Assume" statements. The output assertion is a "Prove" statement.

0		*Assume (Real (X));*	Input assertions
1		*Assume (Integer (N));*	
2		*Assume (N > 1);*	
3		Real Proc E(X,N);	
4		Real X; Integer N,I;	
5		*Assume (Integer (I));*	Input assertion
6		E ⟵ X;	
7		I ⟵ 1;	
8	Loop:	*Assume (E = X**I);*	Loop Invariant
9		IF (I ⩾ N) GOTO DONE;	
10		E ⟵ E*X;	
11		I ⟵ I + 1;	
12		GOTO Loop;	
13	Done:	*Prove (E = X**N);* END;	Output assertion

First, you break the program into segments which contain no loops, each with its own input and output assertion. Breaking up the program (and the loop), you obtain three segments, as shown below.

Segment 1, the first entry to the loop, is

0	*Assume (Real (X));*
1	*Assume (Integer (N));*
2	*Assume (N ⩾ 1);*

5   *Assume (Integer (I));*
6   E ◄——— X;
7   I ◄——— 1;
8   *Prove (E = X**I);*

Segment 2, the Ith time through the loop, is

8   *Assume (E = X**I);*
9   *Assume (I < N);*
10   E ◄——— E *X;
11   I ◄——— I + 1;
8   *Prove (E = X**I);*

Segment 3, the exit path from the loop, is

8   *Assume (E = X**I);*
9   *Assume (I ⩾ N);*
13   *Prove (E = X**N);*

You elect to start with the second segment, the "general case" for the loop (it covers all cases for I = 2 through I = N – 1).

The loop invariant is

$$E = X**I$$

That is, the program variables E, X, and I are always in this relation at the top and the bottom of the loop. (Note that " = " means mathematical equality, *not* programming assignment.) Passing this expression back through statement 11 (statement numbers are shown to the left of the program listing) produces the expression

$$E = X**(I + 1)$$

Passing this expression through statement 10 produces

$$E*X = X** (I + 1)$$

Passing this expression through statement 9 produces

$$(I < N) \supset (E*X = X** (I + 1))$$

Thus the condition to be verified for this segment is

$$(E = X^{**}I) \supset [(I < N) \supset (E^*X = X^{**}(I+1))]$$

which can be rewritten as

$$[(E = X^{**}I) \wedge (I < N)] \supset (E^*X = X^{**}(I+1))$$

[This states that if we know that E is equal to X raised to the Ith power and I is less than N, it must follow that E times X is equal to X raised to the (I + 1)th power.] (I < N) is not needed for the proof. Multiplying both sides of

$$E = X^{**}I$$

by X and with a little algebra you get the right-hand side of the implication, and the condition to be verified is shown to be correct.

With only a little knowledge of proof-of-correctness techniques, you feel intimidated by the process. You decide to use the technique only on the highly mathematical and relatively straightforward segments of your bookmaking program.

REFERENCES

1. "An Introduction to Proving the Correctness of Programs," *ACM Computing Surveys,* Sept., 1976; Hantler and King.

Presents a tutorial on proof methodologies. Discusses the use of symbolic execution to assist with simple programs, and inductive assertion for less simple ones. Shows example proofs.

2. "A Summary of Progress Toward Proving Program Correctness," *Proceedings of the Fall Joint Computer Conference, 1972* (published by AFIPS Press); Linden.

States that proof of correctness is feasible for small, critical modules of a large system but is not likely to be cost-effective for routine programs in the near future. Illustrates proof using the same example as this section. Discusses possible automation of proofs.

3. "Proving Program Correctness," *Software Reliability,* Wiley–Inter-science, 1976; Myers.

States that "the entire concept of proving program correctness is of no practical use today," but leaves hopes for the future. Discusses the methodology by example, and itemizes its strengths and weaknesses.

4. "Social Processes and Proofs of Theorems and Programs," *Proceedings of Fourth Symposium on Principles of Programming Languages, 1977;* DeMillo, Lipton, and Perlis.

Takes the unusual position that mathematical proofs require an elaborate social process to achieve both rigor and acceptance. Suggests that program proofs are unlikely to be supported in this way and are thus unlikely to become of practical value.

3.4.2   Testing methods

There is a serious software reliability dichotomy between what should be and what is.

Ideally, intense use of software reliability techniques in the early phases of software development, as discussed in previous sections, should eliminate or minimize problem occurrence later. Rigorously wrung-out requirements, thorough and detailed specifications, intelligent and thoughtful design, and careful implementation should result, in theory, in an immediately useful software product.

Such is far from the case. Typically, the bulk of software reliability work occurs in the testing phase, wherein attempt after partially successful attempt is made to get the newly produced software to execute correctly on reasonably simple input data. It seems to be human nature, at least using past reliability methodology, to err—and frequently.

It is interesting to note that it is also human nature to expect not to err. A favorite trick played on novice programmers newly emerged from the academic world is to bet them that their first program will *not* work correctly on its first test try. Experienced programmers have been known to gain some measure of wealth preying on the naive expectations of green programmers, whose work is, surprisingly (to them), subject to the frailties of us all!

Regardless of the care undertaken in the earlier phases of development, it will be necessary to test—and test hard—to achieve reliable software. No advancement in reliability technology—either state-of-the-art or on-the-horizon—is going to change that situation significantly, although many will chip away at it. Knowledge of testing techniques is an essential part of the programmer's tool kit.

Testing itself may be broken down into several phases or levels of usage. In traditional bottom-up development techniques, individual small program components are tested at the *unit test* level before being assembled into the software whole. *Integration testing,* using the fully joined software product, is the next level of testing; and finally, for "embedded computer" systems, where the computer is part of a larger system (e.g., the flight computer in an airplane), *system testing* is the final level of test. Even for top-down programming, where the integration phase is largely eliminated (see Section 3.3.1), testing proceeds through levels as more and more code stubs are replaced with legitimate code.

Although testing itself is an ancient and reasonably well understood process, the application of testing to the previously discussed phases is not. Particularly for large computer systems, involving a large number of programmers and large quantities of code, the processes of integration and system testing are ill-defined and extremely ad hoc. The state of the art cannot yet clarify which testing tools are useful for top-level testing and not for unit testing, and vice versa. Most test tool research and development, in fact, has occurred at the unit test level simply because it is better understood and easier to simulate in the research environment. The eager reader is urged to file away in the back of his mind the unmet need for improved integration/system testing techniques; this is a field in which contributions over the next few years will be extremely valuable.

Testing is the execution of software to determine where it functions incorrectly. Testing includes deliberately constructing difficult sets of input data designed to maximize the possibility of software failure. What testing should never be is a simplistic application of a minimum number of test cases selected to show only that the software works. Under cost and schedule pressures, it is sometimes tempting to short-circuit the test process in this way. The result is inevitably disaster—unreliable software, unhappy customers, and worse.

The process of going about testing requires planning. In fact, in many environments, particularly U.S. government-sponsored software development, a test plan and test procedures document must be produced prior to the testing itself. Such documentation is discussed in Section 4.3.

There are two complementary forces driving the testing process. From the software customer point of view, testing must demonstrate that all product requirements are met. Test plans and procedures usually stress the definition of a matrix of requirements versus test cases, sufficient to show that all requirements are covered by at least one test case.

However, from the programmer point of view, testing must demonstrate that all components of the structure of the software are executed. The construction of odd-ball test cases is usually done to force the test execution of some obscure portion of a program otherwise untestable. As experienced programmers know only too well, it is the exceptional case that often consumes the most programming time, is the most difficult to test, and is the most often wrong. The simplicity of classroom exercises often stems directly from the omission of such exceptions; it is this lack of reality in academic software exercises (the outside world is unfortunately full of exceptions) which gives rise to the expression *real-world programming,* meaning consideration of a problem complete with all its warts and wrinkles, as opposed to *academic programming.* Be warned that a most difficult and important part of testing is the ferreting out of problems in obscure, exception structures.

Thus we have *requirements-driven* testing, and *structure-driven* testing. Note that neither is sufficient without the other. If a requirement is not satisfied, structure-driven testing may not detect it, since the corresponding software structure may also be omitted; and if a piece of structure is wrong, explicit requirements testing may well not detect it, since requirements are seldom detailed enough to account for all pieces of software structure (i.e., requirements do not dictate, except very indirectly, all the IF-THEN-ELSEs of a program).

Traditionally, then, testing is a blending:

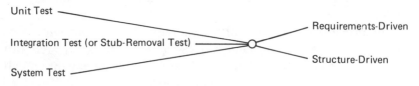

Figure 3.7

controlled overall by a test plan and procedures document. Below the level of the preceding discussion, it is largely ad hoc. The material that follows discusses some specific tools and techniques, many of them not yet in common use, which can add rigor to that still ad hoc process.

REFERENCES

1. "Hints on Test Data Selection: Help for the Practicing Programmer," *Computer (IEEE),* Apr., 1978; DeMillo, Lipton, and Sayward.

Makes a strong case for the use of an intuitive, ad hoc approach to testing, on the grounds that other approaches reject the truism that most programs under test are "nearly correct."

2. "A Controlled Experiment in Program Testing and Code Walkthroughs/Inspections," Communications of the ACM, Sept., 1978; Myers.

Finds testing to be subject to individual variability, and alarmingly inadequate by itself. Suggests (1) complementing testing with peer code reviews, and (2) use of two independently-operating testers.

3.4.2.1   SOURCE LANGUAGE DEBUG

Source language debug is the process of debugging a program via the programming language in which it is coded rather than in the computer's machine language.

To make clear what source language debug is, it will help to illustrate what it is not. Historically, program debugging has occurred as described in the following scenario.

The newly coded program, returned from keypunch in punched card form or submitted to a timesharing file via a remote terminal console and file editor system, is ready for a debug run. A test case is constructed, using sample representative input data, and the job control information necessary to tell the computer what to do with the program and its data is also built. This total package—program, job control, and input data—is then submitted to the computer for execution. If the submittal is via punched cards, the deck is carried to a batch card input area and left for subsequent computer entry by computer operations personnel; if the submittal is via timesharing, the new information is keyed in via the terminal, the program file is requested, and execution begins largely transparent to operational personnel. In either case, in the typical situation, the debug run aborts: it causes the computer operating system to detect an impossible condition and terminate the job. Even if the run does not abort, it may run to completion with absurd or nonexistent output.

The programmer's dilemma at this point is to find out what went wrong, and where. In the case of an abort, the operating system probably printed out descriptive information automatically to assist the programmer. However, typically this information is in machine code form. Since an operating system supports many different languages, there is no way for it to know what programming language the programmer understands in order to play back the necessary information in human-readable form. Therefore, its only choice is to print the information in the only form it is sure of—machine code, which, depending on the computer, may be hexadecimal or octal numbers, or character-string equivalents of the numerical form, or both. The information printed will probably include the location in computer memory at which the abort occurred, perhaps a history of the locations of preceding subroutine/procedure calls, and a dump of some or all of computer memory.

Now consider the plight of the programmer. If his run aborted, he is confronted with pages of effective gibberish. In order to read this information, he must be able to convert large numbers from hex or octal to decimal, know where in computer memory various components of his program's instructions and data reside, and perhaps even decode numeric data into the corresponding computer instruction or floating-point number or character string or bit string. These are all nontrivial jobs, each requiring an elaborate learning process of its own.

If the programmer's run did not abort, he may be in even worse shape. Although he has no gibberish to decode, he has nothing at all to assist him in defining what went wrong.

Debugging is like reading a murder mystery. The programmer/reader keeps a sharp eye out for clues which, coupled with his knowledge of his program, enable him to realize what portion of the program is the guilty malfunctioner. The problem here is that the clues are either in a foreign language, or nearly nonexistent.

Enter the crime lab of computing! Source language debug transforms the preceding scenario into the one that follows, using debug methodology as modern as the language in which the programmer coded his job.

The preparation of the job submittal takes place largely as before. The program, the job control, and the sample input are prepared in an appropriate medium. However, at some time prior to job submittal, one more pass is made over the program and job control, inserting invocations of source debug capabilities. These are typically computer-system-dependent but may take the form of (1) special output statements in the program, printing key data in formatted form for debug analysis; (2) abort-triggered calls to a postmortem formatted dump program, embedded in the program or its job control; (3) trace statements in the program, printing program structure points executed and/or data variables as their values are changed, complete with name and value (if any), formatted for ease of readability; (4) calls to formatted snapshot dump routines in the program, where the dump also includes variable names and formatted values and, additionally, prints only those variables whose value has changed since the last snapshot; (5) debug on/off statements in the program which suppress or enable the specified debug actions at compile time so that source language debug statements may be left in a program's source code but turned off until they are needed.

Following the insertion of these debug statements in the program and its job control, the program is again executed. The output story, now, is totally different from before. If the run aborts, the abort is preceded by an "audit trail" of data and logic printouts, saying what has happened as the program executed, in the order in which it happened. The abort itself is accompanied by a human-readable memory dump. If the run does not abort, the audit trail is of course still present, and the programmer may ascertain more precisely what the program did and did not do as it executed.

Now the programmer-sleuth has an effective and usable set of clues to work from. Not only does the computer speak to him, even in times of trouble, in his own language; better yet, he has been able to preplan the output clues he would really like to have to assist his debug process. Bear in mind that prior to a computer test run, the programmer usually does not know that a "crime" will be committed, or what it will be, or where; but via preplanned source language debug, he can be prepared to research the crime through deliberately implanted clues.

State of the Art in Source Language Debug

The enthusiasm and explicitness of the preceding discussion is somewhat misleading. There are, in fact, few if any commonly used software production systems that have all the capabilities named. (The IBM PL/1 checkout compiler is one of the better ones.) Many systems have pieces of the total system described (e.g., most JOVIAL compilers have a data item and logic control point trace capability). Many others have none (except those which the programmer manually inserts himself). The fact of the matter is that source language debug is not a commonly used, state-of-the-art technique.

There are several reasons for this situation. Perhaps the leading reason is one that is central to the theme of this guidebook—software reliability simply has not had the managerial, financial, and academic attention over the years that other facets of computing have had. The payoff from software productivity aids, such as coding in a high-level language, is obvious and relatively measurable. The payoff from improving the tools used by the programmer to make software more trustworthy is not obvious and not measurable. Only in recent years has interest in reliability technology become high enough among the funding sources in our field to mount a broad attack on the problem areas.

This historic failure is most clearly seen in the source language debug area. The language in which programmers program has received enormous attention over the last two decades. Both the academic and industrial worlds have evolved languages from the primitive early Fortrans and Fargos (an early commercial report generator program) to the highly sophisticated Pascals and PL/1s; yet there has been little corresponding increase in the source language debug capabilities provided in most production compilers and on most commonly used computers. The lack is not for want of knowledge; papers describing such capabilities have been published reasonably plentifully over that same era. There has simply been no force motivating the obvious extension from high-level language coding to high-level language debugging.

Even in the otherwise-respectable requirements definition for the Department of Defense common language Ada,* for example, source language debug capability is dealt with only in the last paragraph and only in passing. No explicit capabilities requirements are included.

Cost of Source Language Debug

Source language debug, as defined here, is a family of related capabilities. Many, but not all of the capabilities must be specially implemented in the language processor—compiler or precompiler—for the language being used. Thus the cost is dependent on a number of factors. If the language processor already exists, it may be rather expensive to add capabilities not present ($25,000 to $100,000 at professional wages and industrial overheads). If the language processor is designed to include source language debug facilities from the beginning, on the other hand, the incremental cost is fairly trivial.

Not all the capabilities are language/compiler dependent. Special output statements with formatted printout, for example, may usually be programmer-inserted in commonly used languages with no language change necessary. Abort-triggered calls to postmortem formatted dumps are an operating system dependency, with additional costs analogous to those for computer changes. But all the other capabilities—trace statements, snapshot dumps, and debug on/off—are a function of the compiler and its support library. (A precompiler that translates debug constructs into compilable language is also a possible approach, but preprocessors tend to introduce one more level of separation between what the programmer coded and what is being checked out.)

---

*"Department of Defense Requirements for High Order Computer Programming Languages (Steelman)," June, 1978. Available through Lt. Col. William A. Whitaker, Defense Advanced Research Projects Agency, 1400 Wilson Blvd. Arlington, Va. 22209.

Example of Source Language Debug

The following source language debug invocations show specific examples of the syntactic and semantic forms that source language debug capabilities might take.

Special Output Statements

    PUT NAMED ALPHA, BETA, GAMMA;
    PUT NAMED COMMON__FILE__1;

These output requests would result in printouts of the form

    ALPHA = 1.2E2, BETA = − 12, GAMMA = ABCDEFG
    COMMON__FILE__1:
    ITEM1 = 1.2E0, ITEM2 = 1.6E-1, ITEM3 = 7, ITEM4 = 7A00F

where the name of the variable and its value, formatted according to its declaration, are printed at the time the PUT statement is executed.

Note that the PUT request for a data aggregate (e.g., COMMON __FILE__1) produces a printout of each of the components.

Name-directed output such as this is available in a few languages (e.g., PL/1). In languages where the capability for automatic name printout is not available, the programmer may include it in a format statement accompanying a WRITE:

    WRITE ALPHA, BETA, GAMMA;
    FORMAT ('ALPHA = ',E, 'BETA = ',I, 'GAMMA = ',C);

Trace Statements

    TRACE ALPHA, BETA, GAMMA;

This executable statement will cause a printout of the form

    ALPHA = 1.2E2

to occur each time the value of any of the named variables subsequently changes during program execution.

    TRACE PROCEDURE1, LABEL1;

112

This executable statement will cause a printout of the form

    PROCEDURE1

to occur each time the named procedure or label is subsequently entered.

    TRACE FLOW;

This executable statement will cause a record to be kept at execute-time of the most recent logic branchout statements (e.g., GOTO, CALL), so that they can be printed at the termination of execution, or during execution, or both.

    DETRACE ALPHA; or DETRACE LABEL1; or DETRACE FLOW;

These executable statements will dynamically suppress the named tracing.

Formatted Snapshot Dumps

    SNAP ALPHA, BETA, GAMMA;

This statement will cause the value of the named variables to be printed in a manner completely analogous to PUT NAMED, but only if the value of the variable has been changed since the last such snapshot printout.

    SNAP ALL;

This statement will cause all the program's variables to be printed. It is especially useful if it is specified to be executed on any abnormal halt (e.g., SNAP ALL ON HALT).

Debug On/Off

    DEBUG ON;

This statement takes effect at compile time and causes all subsequent debug statements to be processed by the compiler.

    DEBUG OFF;

The statement causes all subsequent debug statements to be ignored by the compiler.

In any given program, it is unlikely that the programmer would make use of all of these capabilities, since there is some overlap between them. A typical mix might include SNAP ALL ON HALT (for unexpected terminations), TRACE FLOW (for logic flow), and DEBUG ON/OFF (to control the insertion/deletion of debug statements at compile time).

REFERENCES

1.   "Debugging Tools for High-Level Languages," *Software—Practice and Experience,* 1972; Sotterthwaite.

Presents the case for source language debug, then describes a system implemented in support of an Algol W compiler. Tracing, postmortem summaries and dumps, execution path counts (a built-in test coverage analyzer), and assertions (see Section 3.4.2.3) are provided. Implementation concepts using interpreter packages which operate off compiled code are described. Resource costs of the capabilities are dealt with.

2.   "A 1900 Fortran Post Mortem Dump System," *Software—Practice and Experience,* July 1978; Ng and Young.

Describes a source language debug tool which produces Fortran language dumps (optionally) on program termination. Includes symbolically identified data and some execution history data. Interfaces with the compiler, linker and a PMD analyzer.

3.   "OS PL/1 Checkout Compiler Programmer's Guide" (for the IBM 370), SC330007.

Describes the use of the PL/1 checkout compiler, including its source language debug capabilities.

4.   "SPLINTER—A PL/1 Interpreter Emphasizing Debugging Capability," *Computer Bulletin,* Sept., 1968; Glass.

An interpretive implementation of a scientific subset of PL/1 is discussed. Source language debug capabilities are described, including data/logic tracing and mathematical significance tracing. Implementation techniques and the cost of an interpreter are also covered.

3.4.2.2   TEST COVERAGE ANALYZER

When a program is undergoing test, it is important to know which portions of the program have been tested and which have not. An emerging tool that allows the measurement of this criteria is called the test coverage analyzer.

A *test coverage analyzer* is a computer program which, when applied to another computer program (the "subject program"), provides for counting each occurrence of the execution of each logic segment of the subject program.

To perform this task, the analyzer program must examine the subject program and divide it into structural members small enough to make the analysis worthwhile and yet large enough to avoid inundating the subject programmer with data. Typically, this division is at the level of logic branches. The code between any two such branch points may be called a decision-to-decision segment; each logic branch in a program causes two or more such segments to begin. A logic branch is a statement such as GOTO, IF, or CASE which causes program flow to divert from the normal sequential process.

Having dissected a program into segments, the analyzer then "instruments" each one. Instrumentation in this case is the process of adding code to the subject program which provides for tallying each instance of execution of that segment. Those tallies will be recorded (as the program executes) in a small data base which the analyzer must also append to the subject program. At the conclusion of execution, the data base must be printed out. An analyzer postprocessor program provides this capability.

Thus the analyzer is actually a kind of superstructure in which test runs are embedded. The subject program is instrumented by it, its data base records the desired information, and its postprocessor operates after the run.

Given all this methodology, what, in fact, does an analyzer do for you?

Suppose that you are a programmer and have just produced a Fortran program which is undergoing test. Suppose further that you have constructed a half-dozen test cases which you believe fairly comprehensively wring out your code. You have carefully tested every requirement levied on you by your customer, but you still have the nagging suspicion that there are byways in your program which remain untested. (If you don't have that nagging suspicion, you are naive!)

Now you consider the analyzer. Knowing that it can relate the structure of your program to execution counts as your program runs, you decide to make use of one. What you intend to do is measure the "testedness" of your program when your test cases are run against it. *What you are really doing is measuring the effectiveness of the test cases by analyzing the program.*

You input your source code to the analyzer just as if it were input data. The analyzer reads it in and outputs a modified version of your code containing the instrumentation code previously described. This augmented source is then fed into the Fortran compiler. The resulting object code is link-loaded, and in addition to the library routines your program already needed, a few special analyzer library routines, and the analyzer data base, are linked into your loadable program.

You are now ready to execute the instrumented code. What you have is a version of your program, identical to what you coded in all other functional respects, but with the added capability of measuring itself (and, as a result, your test cases) as it executes.

One by one, you input your test cases. As each runs, your program outputs (in addition to the output you provided for) a table showing each segment of your program and the count of the number of times it was executed.

The most interesting things in this table are the zero-count segments, because they are the ones not executed by that particular test case. As each test case runs, you get another table, showing the impact of *that* test case on segment execution frequency counts. If, at the conclusion of all the test cases, there are one or more segments for which the count is zero for all tests, then clearly there is a portion of your program not yet tested.

If there is such a zero-count segment, your work has just begun. Obviously, you would like to either build a test case to force an execution of that segment or at least understand why it was not executed. Perhaps it is an unexecutable, useless code. More likely, it is exception case code for a facet of the program's capability not yet tested. In any case, your job now is to go back to the program source code, find out what the function of the untested segment is, and decide what to do about it.

Analyzer usage, then, may become an iterative process—instrument, execute, inspect results, inspect the program, revise the test, and repeat. The analyzer is, quite literally, a tool, by means of which more can be learned about the testedness of a program, in order to decide whether to and how to improve that testedness.

There are other benefits to the use of an analyzer, not all of them reliability-related. Since the analyzer relates program segments to test cases that execute them, it is possible to reduce the testing of a revised program to those test cases which test only the revised portions. Also, high-frequency counts for program segments are a clue pointing to portions of a program that perhaps should become candidates for optimization (that is a reliability consideration to the extent that premature code optimization sometimes leads to unreliable programs, and the frequency count technique is an effective way of deferring optimization to a more meaningful time).

Analyzers are by no means a reliability cure-all, however. Although dissecting a program into its constituent logic segments is a fairly rigorous approach to structural testing, ideally the analysis should take into account *all combinations* of such segments. Frequently, it is not an untested segment, but an untested sequence of tested segments, which hides a latent programming error. Such a level of analysis, however, is infeasible by today's technology. The combinatorial mathematics of a program of any magnitude quickly makes the number of individual sequences of segments astronomical. Thus the analyzer as we presently know it is a compromise. Note that other compromises are possible—for the integration of large programs, or for programs where the sizing and timing impact of the instrumentation is prohibitive, it may be preferable to segment the program into procedure invocations, for example; the rigor of the analysis is lessened considerably, but the manageability of the resulting data is increased. Such a "coarse-grain analyzer" might be useful for real-time applications, for example, where instrumentation-caused distortions in program execution time might prevent the program from executing successfully.

Another possible compromise is the computer hardware analyzer, which can monitor the instruction counter of a CPU and can provide statistics at that level without impacting sizing and timing. This technique is especially useful for micro and real-time computing, where sizing/timing may be critical. Statistics at that level, however, are sometimes difficult to track back to the source code level, and a thorough hardware analysis of a class of constructs (e.g., all branches) is hard to implement.

A study was conducted at the Boeing Aerospace Company to estimate what percentage of program errors might be isolated and corrected by rigorous use of an analyzer, forcing the traverse of all segments in the search for program errors. In a population of three fairly mature programs of mixed complexity (one was a compiler) and during the reporting of about 50 errors, the findings were: about 25% of the errors would have been found by appropriate analyzer usage; 40% would only have been found by an analyzer that examined all combinations of logic segments; and the remaining 35% were errors of omission, and thus also not subject to analyzer-aided detection. As stated before, the analyzer is not a reliability cure-all, and this study supports that statement. As with other reliability tools, its use merely increases the chance that the software so processed will be reliable.

State of the Art in Test Coverage Analyzers

Analyzers are a relatively new concept; research into the area began less than a decade ago. Analyzers are not commonly used. The number of analyzers actually implemented is limited to a handful, and many are proprietary to the developing company. McDonnell-Douglas Astronautics, for example, makes heavy use of its Program Evaluator and Tester (PET) on in-house Fortran software development; and the Air Force has procured JAVS, the JOVIAL language Automated Verification System, for DoD project usage. However, one leading implementor of analyzers for sale to other companies does not, in fact, use analyzers on in-house developmental efforts (because of the work involved in analyzing the results). Thus there is a mixed picture regarding the use and effectiveness of analyzers.

Some analyzers augment the basic segment-count capability with related reliability support tools. JAVS, for example, produces an analysis of the logic paths which must be traversed to execute an untested segment in order to assist the user in constructing improved test cases. PET gathers execution profile data describing such things as the ranges of data variables during execution, the number of subroutine calls that were executed, and the percent of the total number of subroutines that were called.

The implementation of contemporary analyzers is language-dependent. An analyzer processes one and only one language, typically operating before the compiler as a preprocessor, translating the user's source into an instrumented source still compatible with the language. It would be possible, and perhaps preferable, to build the analyzer capability into a compiler, but this has seldom been done (the ALGOL W compiler is an exception).

Cost of Test Coverage Analyzer

Availability is the key to the cost of an analyzer. If one has been implemented for the language you are using, on the computer you are using, the cost may range from free to a few thousand dollars.

If an analyzer is not available and must be implemented, the cost increment is significant. A simple coarse-grain analyzer, as discussed previously, might cost $20,000 to implement (at professional wages and industrial overheads). A full logic path analyzer, with no other capability, might cost $75,000. But a complex analyzer, with added capabilities such as those of PET or JAVS, will cost upward of $250,000.

In addition to acquisition costs, there are ongoing costs to analyzer usage. The instrumentation added to a program by the analyzer has a significant sizing and timing impact on the resulting code. The study described in Section 3.6.2 indicates that the memory requirements of a program may grow by 2 to 45%, and its execution time may grow by a factor of from 1.1:1 to 8.5:1. Such impacts obviously have strong leverage on decisions regarding analyzer usage. Human costs, also, may be significant. It is not costly to set up an analyzer run. But analysis of the results, particularly if the user attempts to augment his testing to cover all logic segments, will be expensive.

The trade-offs of analyzer usage, as with all reliability tools, are to compare the reliability benefits of the use of the tool with the costs. This is no easy task; one of the serious problems with reliability technology is that the dollar value of its benefits is purely hypothetical.

Examples of Test Coverage Analyzer

The listings below show a simple source program before and after instrumenting and then show the table of segment counts produced when the program is executed.

Source Program

```
RANDOM SMALL, RANDOM_LARGE= 0;
FOR I = 1 TO 1000 BY 1;
BEGIN "CATEGORIZE RANDOM NUMBERS"
  GET_RANDOM_NUMBER (RESULT);
  IF 0 ≤ RESULT ≤ .5
  THEN RANDOM_SMALL = RANDOM_SMALL + 1;
  ELSE RANDOM_LARGE = RANDOM_LARGE + 1;
END "CATEGORIZE RANDOM NUMBERS"
PUT NAMED RANDOM_SMALL,RANDOM_LARGE;
STOP;
END
```

Source Program, After Instrumentation

```
COUNT_SEGMENT(1); "*ANALYZER CALL*"
RANDOM_SMALL, RANDOM_LARGE = 0;
FOR I = 1 TO 1000 BY 1;
BEGIN "CATEGORIZE RANDOM NUMBERS"
  COUNT_SEGMENT(2); "*ANALYZER CALL*"
  GET_RANDOM NUMBER (RESULT);
  IF 0 ≤ RESULT ≤ .5
  THEN BEGIN
    COUNT_SEGMENT(3); "*ANALYZER CALL*"
    RANDOM_SMALL = RANDOM_SMALL + 1;
    END
  ELSE BEGIN
    COUNT_SEGMENT(4); "*ANALYZER CALL*"
    RANDOM_LARGE = RANDOM_LARGE + 1;
    END
END "CATEGORIZE RANDOM NUMBERS"
COUNT_SEGMENT(5); "*ANALYZER CALL*"
PUT NAMED RANDOM_SMALL, RANDOM_LARGE;
PRINT_SEGMENT_COUNTS; "*ANALYZER CALL*"
STOP;
END
```

Analyzer Output, After Execution (Program Output Not Shown)

SEGMENT NUMBER VS. EXECUTION FREQUENCIES

UNITS ⟶	1	2	3	4	5	6	7	8	9
TENS ↓									
0	-	1	1000	475	525	1	-	-	-	-

The matrix contents are the number of times each segment was executed. For example, segments 1 and 5, outside the loop, were executed once; and segments 2, 3, and 4, inside the loop, were executed 1000, 475, and 525 times, respectively.

REFERENCES

1. "An Approach to Program Testing," *ACM Computing Surveys,* Sept., 1975; Huang.

Tutorial paper which analyzes the difficulties of rigorous testing; suggests the test coverage analyzer concept as a solution, and discusses the usage, strengths, and weaknesses of such a tool.

2. "Software Testing: Principles and Practice Using a Testing Coverage Analyzer," *Transactions of the Software '77 Conference,* Oct., 1977; Paige.

Testing is called "the most practical means to demonstrate software correctness." The notion of a testing analyzer is defined and illustrated, with sample analyzer outputs shown. Testing strategies using an analyzer are discussed.

3. "A Verification Case Study," *Proceedings of the AIAA Computers in Aerospace Conference, 1977;* Gannon.

Describes the JOVIAL Automated Verification System (JAVS) and its use. The self-test of JAVS using JAVS as part of its government acceptance testing is discussed. Conclusions about the effectiveness of test coverage analyzers are drawn.

4. "A User's Appraisal of an Automated Program Verification Aid," AFAL-TR-75-242, 1975; Whipple and Pitts.

Discusses the strengths and weaknesses of RXVP, a Fortran-automated verification system which includes test coverage analyzer capabilities. Concludes: "The utility of automated tools . . . will depend to a great extent on congruence between the views of testing held by the tool developer and the tool user,'' and that testing is and will continue to be an art.

3.4.2.3   ASSERTION CHECKER

Preplanning the debugging process has historically been a problem for programmers. The impatient programmer, hard charging toward what his optimism tells him will be his first and last test run, finds it very difficult to stop and contemplate the possibility that this first run will, in fact, fail and that he should prepare for it.

Source language debug, as we have seen in an earlier section, provides some capabilities for the anticipating programmer. The concept of assertion checking is a more rigorous approach to this problem.

An assertion is a statement of what is presumed to be fact. In a computing sense, it is a statement that should hold true as a program executes. A "local" assertion is one that should hold true at the point of declaration; a "global" assertion is one that should hold true throughout program execution.

An assertion checker is a tool that provides for the evaluation of assertions during program execution, and records their truth or falsity. Note that the concept of assertions is also important to the proof-of-correctness process; however, the assertion checker is a dynamic test tool, only mildly related to the static proof process.

Observe the experienced programmer as he incorporates the assertion checker capability into his careful pretest planning:

Having finished inserting his source language debug statements— snapshots, postmortem dumps, etc.—the programmer makes one more pass over his source code, contemplating the assertions he is able to make about it.* First and foremost, he will specify the legitimate range of all variables in his program; the assertion checker, he knows, will provide for the detection of any violation of those range limitations. Further, he may specify discrete legitimate or illegitimate values a variable may have. Perhaps the constituents of a data array

---

*Better yet, the planning for source language debug and (especially) assertions should have occurred in the design phase and will have materialized in the code on that basis.

must possess a certain interrelationship, such as being in ascending order; he will specify that. Or certain constituents of an array have particular limitations on legitimate subscript values; that, too, he will specify. If a subprogram can have (or not have) side effects, they can be stated. He examines his program with a specific set of assertions—those the assertion checker is prepared to deal with—in mind. For each, he adds special assertion code to his program.

Until now, there has been no similarity between the assertion checker process and the previously mentioned test coverage analyzer. The goals are different: the assertion checker is a debug aid (and an important form of documentation); the analyzer measures test case adequacy. The method of usage is different: the assertion checker requires additions to the program, the analyzer allows its user to be passive, making no change.

The gross dissimilarity of the two tools now ends, however. As with the analyzer, the programmer inputs his source code to the assertion checker, just as if it were input data. The assertion checker reads it in and outputs a modified version of the code containing the instrumentation code corresponding to the programmer's assertions. This augmented code is then fed into the compiler. The resulting object code is link-loaded, and in addition to the library routines his program already needed, a few special assertion library routines, and an assertion data base, are linked into the loadable program. (The alert reader will see that this wording is identical to that in the analyzer section, except for the substitution of "assertion" for "analyzer.")

The programmer is now ready to execute the instrumented code. In the case of the assertion checker, of course, the instrumentation corresponds directly to the programmer-inserted assertion rather than the system-inserted logic path code as with the analyzer. What the programmer has is a version of his program, identical to what he coded in all other respects but with the added capability of detecting assertion violations (and, for that matter, nonviolations), reporting individual violations, and summarizing the total assertion violation/ success statistics for the run.

As he runs his test cases, the programmer gets, in addition to his normal output and his source language debug output, a record of assertion action. Consider the value of any assertion violation messages which the prorammer may receive—he learns facts that normal debugging techniques might not tell him until much later. Unless a variable being out of range causes some other symptom such as an abort, for example, the programmer might not be aware that his program was malfunctioning without the aid of the assertion checker. Thus the assertion checker is an early warning tool, aggressively seeking out error situations rather than waiting for them to happen.

State of the Art in Assertion Checkers

The assertion checker concept is fairly new. Very few assertion checker systems have been implemented, and no industrial environment usage on a broad scale is known. In one experiment in their use as part of a graduate-level computer science course at UCLA, definite improvements were noted in program testing time, with some surprising fringe benefits in program quality. The experiment population was small, however, and no other data are known.

As with analyzers, implementation of assertion checkers is language-dependent. Since assertions are programmer-inserted into a program, their form must be compatible with the language being used. Either a preprocessor approach, or an in-compiler implementation, is possible. The latter is preferable (for ease of use, lower implementation costs, and eliminating the separation between the programmer's code and that which he is checking out), but, again as with analyzers, it is not commonly done because language specifications rarely include syntax for assertions, and thus compiler implementations do not provide for them (ALGOL W, here again, is an exception).

Local assertions may also be programmer-inserted using conventional techniques and without benefit of an assertion checker [e.g., IF NOT (.01 < A < 1.0) THEN ASSERTION_VIOLATION(A);]; however, the coding is cumbersome and must occur frequently in the code. There is no convenient corresponding option for global assertions, of course.

Cost of Assertion Checker

Since there are few assertion checkers available, there is virtually no way to avoid the high implementation cost if one is desired. Construction of a preprocessor is likely to cost at least $75,000. Building the assertion checker into a compiler will be less if the implementor is familiar with the internals of the compiler; otherwise, considerably more.

There are usage costs as well as acquisition costs. The analysis necessary to insert assertions into a program is nontrivial. How does the programmer, for example, learn enough about the legitimate range of each of his program's variables to make the range declarations reasonably rigorous? And of course when a program executes and assertion violations are detected, analysis is necessary to research and correct those conditions. Since the latter time is directly related to error correction (unless the assertion was wrong), it is really not a cost specific to assertion checkers, however.

Although there are no data to prove this, it seems fairly obvious that the value of usage of an assertion checker would be considerably more than its usage costs.

Examples of Assertion Checker

The example data below illustrate (1) the form assertion statements inserted into a program might take, and (2) sample outputs which might result from those assertions.

Sample Assertion Statements

These assertion statements are coded using a distinctive syntax for ease of preprocessor recognition; in these examples, each statement is preceded by an exclamation mark. The assertions are divided into three classes—global assertions (those which must be valid throughout the program's execution), local assertions (those which must be valid at the point encountered), and assertion control (directives controlling how the assertions are to be used).

Global Assertions

!RANGE (list of variables) (minimum value, maximum value)
Correct values of the list of variables must lie between the stated bounds.
!VALUES (list of variables) (list of legal values)
Correct values of the list of variables are only those in the list of values.
!VALUES (list of variables) NOT (list of illegal values)
Correct values of the list of variables are all those not in the illegal list.

!MONITOR (list of variables to be traced)
Variables in the list are to be printed whenever their values change.
!SUBSCRIPT RANGE (list of subscriptable entity, subscript bounds)
Correct subscripts for entities in the list must fall between the stated bounds.

Local Assertions

!RELATION (expression that must be true)
The stated relationship must be true.
!CALL (variables not to be changed by the following subfunction call)
The listed variables must be unchanged following the subfunction call.

Assertion Control

!TRACE ALL
Print a record of all assertions executed, violations or not.
!TRACE FIRST n
Print a record of the first n assertion violations to occur.
!TRACE LAST n
Print a record of the last n assertion violations to occur.
!TRACE ON (violation list)
Print all occurrences of the listed violations (e.g., RANGE, VALUES, etc.)
!TRACE OFF (violation list)
Do not check for the listed violations.
!MONITOR ON (list of variables)
Monitor (see above) variables in the list—dynamically executed.
!MONITOR OFF (list of variables)
Cease monitoring variables in the list—dynamically executed.

Outputs resulting from programmer-coded assertions could include the following:

During-Execution Outputs

!!!ASSERTION *(kind)* (VIOLATION) PROGRAM *(name)*, LINE *(number)*
                    (OK   )
(specifics of the occurrence, such as variable name and value)
!!!MONITOR *(variable name)* = *(value)*, PROGRAM *(name)*, LINE *(number)*

Postexecution Outputs

***ASSERTION *(kind)* SUMMARY, PROGRAM *(name)*, LINE *(number)*
(number) VIOLATIONS, *(number)* OK
***ASSERTION TOTALS FOR THIS RUN -
(number) VIOLATIONS, *(number)* OK

REFERENCES

1. "New Assertion Concepts for Self Metric Software Validation," *Proceedings of the 1975 IEEE International Conference on Reliable Software;* Stucki and Foshee.

The PET (program evaluator and test) system used at McDonnell-Douglas is described. Emphasis is placed on the PET assertion capabilities, although its analyzer and other functions are also described. Examples of assertions imbedded in Fortran program listings are given, with attendant output shown.

2. "A Methodology for Program Verification," *Summer Computer Simulation Conference, 1977;* Saib, Benson, and Melton.

Advocates a comprehensive verification methodology, including assertion checking along with static analysis and a test coverage analyzer. Assertions cover input versus output arguments, units consistency, and logical relationships.

3.4.2.4 TEST DRIVER

Programs are often implemented as building blocks. As each block is programmed, it is tested to determine its validity before being added to the software structure it is to become part of. Since the building block is not a complete program in itself, some "scaffolding" code is necessary to allow it to be tested. This scaffolding is known as a test driver.

A *test driver* is a computer program developed to enable the testing of another computer program or component of a program. In a sense, it is a simulator of the environment in which the component will actually be run. The test driver "drives" what is often called a *unit test,* meaning a test at the component level. (The opposite of a unit test is an *integration test,* a test of the total structure of a program.) The driver enables the inputting of data sufficient to test the components, and the printing of the resulting component outputs.

Test drivers are a vital part of the bottom-up software development method, defined in Section 3.3.1. They are also one of the extra costs which top-down advocates cite as a disadvantage of the bottom-up method. Drivers are essentially "throwaway" code—once the unit test is complete, they may be discarded (unless there is some reason to believe the unit test will need to be repeated later—if the requirements for the component are modified, for example). In the top-down method, the overall program structure exists from the beginning of development and serves as a live driver for newly added code. There is, however, an analogy to the throwaway driver in the top-down method—the stub, a piece of (usually) throwaway dummy code placed in the program structure as a temporary expedient until the real code for that component is developed. Stubs are explained further in Section 3.3.1.

State of the Art in Test Drivers

The test driver concept is as old as programming, and it is heavily used. Even the recent interest in top-down approaches has made little impact on the time-honored tradition of test drivers. Whether that will continue to be true in the future remains to be seen.

Frequently, the test driver is a program that tests a component subroutine. As such, the only language requirement on the driver is that it be able to call the component as a subroutine. Drivers are often coded in "quick and dirty" fashion in a common high-level language with simple yet competent I/O capability, such as Fortran, regardless of the language in which the component is coded.

Some attempts have been made to generalize the test driver problem in order to avoid the cost and waste of producing throwaway code. Test data generators, especially those supporting COBOL-type applications, have been somewhat successful. More general approaches often fail because of the problem of application-specific needs.

Cost of Test Drivers

There is, of course, cost attached to the use of throwaway code, whether it is the bottom-up test driver or the top-down stub. However, this cost is a minor part of overall software development costs on a program of any magnitude, and may be considered nil. (The environment simulator, discussed in the next section, is a form of test driver which is, on the other hand, often quite expensive.)

Examples of Test Driver

Suppose that you are a programmer working on a water fountain simulation system and that you have been asked to code a subroutine to be called SQUIRT. (You were chosen for this assignment because the SQUIRT routine might also prove useful in your elephant simulation.) SQUIRT has inputs of water flow rate and pressure, and outputs the volume of water discharged: SQUIRT (RATE, PRESSURE: VOLUME). Having coded SQUIRT, you then design a test driver;

```
DO UNTIL END-OF-FILE;BEGIN
   READ RATE, PRESSURE;
   SQUIRT (RATE, PRESSURE:  VOLUME);
   PRINT RATE, PRESSURE, VOLUME;
   END
STOP;
```

Using this test driver is a lot of work, especially in comparing output values with "true" output values. Being both smart and lazy, you decide to input the previously computed correct volume for each rate/pressure to make the driver self-checking:

```
DO UNTIL END-OF-FILE; BEGIN
   READ RATE, PRESSURE, VOLUME-IN;
   SQUIRT (RATE, PRESSURE: VOLUME);
   IF VOLUME-IN ≠ VOLUME THEN
      PRINT 'ERROR', RATE, PRESSURE, VOLUME-IN, VOLUME;
   END
STOP;
```

Realizing that you are still testing too small a quantity of input values, you decide to let the driver itself determine a broad spectrum of input cases:

```
FOR RATE = 0 TO 1000 BY .01 BEGIN
   FOR PRESSURE = 0 TO 1000 BY .01 BEGIN
      SQUIRT (RATE, PRESSURE:  VOLUME);
```

```
        PRINT RATE, PRESSURE, VOLUME;
        END
      END
    STOP;
```

(Of course, you now have to go back to manually verifying the output values.)

REFERENCES

1.   RADC-TR-74-300, Structured Programming Series, Vol. 15 (Validation and Verification Study), p. 3-4, May, 1975.

A brief definition is made of the concept of test drivers, together with advantages and disadvantages of their use.

2.   "Automatic Software Test Drivers," *Computer (IEEE),* Apr., 1978; Panzl.

Describes three approaches for the construction of automatic test driver builders, including TPL/2.0, a tool under development at the GE Research and Development Center.

3.   "A Software Testing Control System," *Program Test Methods,* Prentice-Hall, 1973; Youngberg.

An elaborate generalized test controller is described. Capabilities are provided for job control language generation, test data generation, report preparation, and related services. The services and a design for providing them are covered.

3.4.2.5   ENVIRONMENT SIMULATOR

The *environment simulator* is really only a special form of test driver. It is particularly useful in such areas as real-time software development, where the interfacing of the software with some external device must be tested. The word "only" here is misleading, however. Whereas the typical test driver may be a simplistic skeleton, as shown in the preceding section, the typical environment simulator is frequently the opposite. The requirement of an environment simulator to faithfully represent the external world may, indeed, make the simulator more complicated than the program or component being tested. In fact, while the test driver is typically a unit test tool used on a component, the environment simulator may more commonly be used as an integration tool on the total program.

Suppose, as an example, that the SQUIRT subroutine of the previous section is part of a program called FOUNTAIN, which will be used in real time to control an innovative water sculpture in an urban redevelopment area. And suppose, as is commonly the case, that FOUNTAIN and its real-time computer must be checked out and working well before the sculpture itself, or even its water connections, will be complete. Or, if that "suppose" means unrealistic, suppose instead that the expense and risk of putting an untested FOUNTAIN system into an existing water sculpture (what if it allows the pressure to rise too high and wrecks the sculpture, for example) is too high to be allowed.

Then the FOUNTAIN system must be tested outside its intended environment—at least, initially—and an environment simulator for the water sculpture is needed.

The simulator, of course, need not take the form of the sculpture; it only needs to simulate the interfaces between the sculpture and the FOUNTAIN hardware/software system. Still, the fidelity to those interfaces must be exact, since otherwise the test may be too artificial to be of any value.

Because of the complexity of these interfaces and the variety of external stimuli that may be applied to the system under test, a complicated simulation control system called a *scenario* is sometimes needed. The scenario describes what is to happen during the (simulated) test process. It might specify the range of rates and pressures to be applied to FOUNTAIN, for example, including provision for surges of pressure and/or water outages. If the system is sufficiently complex, part of the environment simulator may be a scenario processor, built to allow the user to describe the scenario in human-readable form. A scenario processor is, in effect, a specialized language processor for a scenario input language.

Even more complex environment simulators may include hardware or software components for interface adaptors and/or special simulation consoles. The complexity of the simulator is, of course, totally dependent on the environment being simulated.

One interesting variant of the environment simulator is the *instruction-level simulator* (ILS), a system that allows one computer to simulate another, instruction by instruction. Suppose, for example, that the FOUNTAIN computer is for some reason unavailable when the software is ready for testing. If an ILS for that computer exists which runs on some other computer, the software may be tested there.

Specific complexities aside, the environment simulator is still a test driver at heart—it provides inputs to, and processes outputs from, the software (or hardware/software) system under test.

State of the Art in Environment Simulators

As the applications undertaken by computing specialists become even more complex, the need for and complexity of environment simulators grows apace. The concept is well known, has been around for years, and is frequently used. It is particularly effective in the aerospace world, where computer systems must be well tested before being propelled into space. Since the environment simulator is usually a program test rather than a unit test, the influence of top-down development is not the threat to this concept that it is to test drivers. The question is seldom "Should environment simulation be used?" but more often "How complex must it be?"

It should also be noted here that environment simulators may be ends in themselves, not just test tools. For example, a hardware/software system may be used to train airline pilots in a mockup cab with lifelike stimuli, or to enable the verification of a weapons delivery system which (hopefully) will never be used at all. This type of simulator, however, is beyond the scope of this guidebook.

Cost of Environment Simulators

The cost of an environment simulator will range anywhere from trivial to enormous. As previously stated, it is totally dependent on the system being tested.

Cost of the simulator is seldom a factor in the software decision-making process; usually the decision as to whether the cost is tolerable is made considerably beforehand, at the total system feasibility level. For example, if the cost of the FOUNTAIN simulator is too high, then perhaps the water sculpture itself should not be built, or its schedule revised to simplify or eliminate the need for a simulator.

By the time the system comes under test, it may well be too late to ask the question ''Do we need an environment simulator?''

Most environment simulators are less costly to run than the environment they simulate; otherwise, they would probably not exist. An exception is the previously mentioned instruction-level simulator. Because getting one computer to behave like another at the instruction level is a laborious process (typically the simulating computer is slowed down by a factor of 30 to 150!), this type of simulation is usually used when there is no other alternative—either the simulated computer is not available, or it has inadequate facilities (readers, printers, debuggers, etc.) to support testing.

Examples of Environment Simulators

The previously discussed FOUNTAIN system is one example of an environment simulator. For another example, consider the following.

An Avionics computer system is one that utilizes electronic devices such as computers in an aircraft/spaceship environment. Suppose that you are implementing a real-time Avionics flight control system for a new-generation aircraft which utilizes digital computers and thus software as a control mechanism (earlier systems have used analog computers). The job your software is to perform is to read aircraft system stimuli, such as speed and altitude and direction, and transmit them to pilot-readable instrumentation. Perhaps this instrumentation is a small TV screen and the pilot can select by a pushbutton mechanism which data he wishes displayed (much like a digital watch). Suppose further that the pilot can act on the data you have supplied him by actuating aircraft controls, and the Avionics computer and thus your software has the job of transmitting those pilot inputs to the proper control systems.

Obviously, the external world of your fairly simple program is rather populous. There are pushbuttons and TV screens and sensor inputs and flight mechanism outputs. Perhaps not so obviously, it is totally undesirable to test your software in its intended environment. Not only is there enormous cost to flying an airplane around to test a software system (perhaps thousands of dollars an hour), but there are lives at risk. A program malfunction might actually kill someone. An environment simulator is clearly the right answer.

Your Avionics simulator system, at minimum, must contain capability for inputting speed and altitude and direction, and for outputting that information on some kind of simulated pilot-readable system. It must also have the ability to read simulated pushbutton inputs and transmit that information to simulated control systems. Perhaps these inputs and outputs can be simply card reader in/printer out activities. Or, for more reality and confidence in the system, perhaps a mockup pilot cab and simplistic control replicas are needed. Note that what is spent on the simulator is a function of what is at stake if the software is unreliable. With lives and gross amounts of money at stake, the mockup cab system may well be the right answer.

REFERENCES

1.   "Software Validation of the Titan IIIC Digital Flight Control System Utilizing a Hybrid Computer," *Proceedings of the 1971 Fall Joint Computer Conference;* Jackson and Bravdica.

Describes an elaborate test system built to validate some real-time flight control software. Covers the mission of the total system, the configuration of the test system, the design and development of the software to be tested, and the actual testing of the software in its test system environment.

2.   "Debugging Under Simulation," *Debugging Techniques in Large Systems,* Prentice-Hall, 1971; Supnik.

The concept of instruction-level simulation (ILS) as a debugging tool is described and advocated. Examples of the need for, and usage of, ILS are presented. Specific capabilities of a system called MIMIC are described.

3.4.2.6   TEST DATA GENERATOR

The problem of building an adequate set of test cases is nontrivial. Although the initial test cases fired at a new piece of software are usually simple subsets of the population of possible program inputs, the time must come during the testing process when the test inputs must probe all the obscure nooks and crannies of the program. Manually constructing those test cases becomes harder and harder. The discussion of test case analyzers elsewhere in this section, while exploring means of identifying inadequacies in test cases, leaves open and in fact begs the question of generating adequate test cases.

In the past, test cases have been hand-hewn, specially tailored to the software to be tested. A *test data generator* is a computer program that automatically and systematically constructs test cases.

The problems confronting the generation of test cases, whether manually or automatically, are many. On the one hand, it is desirable to maximize the number of test cases used in order to increase the chance that the program is thoroughly tested. On the other hand, since the construction, execution, and analysis of test cases costs money, it is also desirable to minimize the number of test cases. These two opposing goals can only be met by a carefully chosen set of test cases which cover the necessary ground without needless redundancy.

This is both a positive and a negative factor in doing automated test case generation. It is positive because it involves a complex optimization problem at which computers on occasion excel. It is negative because the very complexity of the problem has so far eluded practical solution except in relatively straightforward cases.

State of the Art in Test Data Generators

Early test data generators were nothing more than sophisticated random-number generators. Although they were able to produce a broad spectrum of inputs, the inputs so produced were not adequately tuned to the problem at hand. As a result, such programs, even when available, were seldom used.

More recent attempts at test data generation have been driven from the content of the program under test itself. Either from structural analysis such as that performed by a test case analyzer, or from programmer-inserted test case generation clues (a "test pattern"), the generator deduces test cases which satisfy the specific test needs of the program. Obviously, there is a great deal of promise in this approach, but it is technologically much more difficult. Again, as a result, such programs are seldom used. However, considerable research is still being conducted in this area.

Cost of Test Data Generators

Since test data generators can occur in a wide variety of forms, their cost can vary accordingly. Acquisition costs might range from a few hundred dollars for an existing random-number-type generator, to major research expenditures to produce a program-content-dependent generator.

Usage costs fluctuate similarly. Simple but not very useful test data generators cost little to use; the more sophisticated type require user participation in the process, either through analysis of program-produced structure diagrams or through insertion of test pattern definitions.

Examples of Test Data Generators

Let us suppose that you have a fairly straightforward report generator, with one structured data file as input, to check out. It is part of the FOUNTAIN simulation system mentioned previously.

You elect to use a random-number-type test data generator. Looking at the required data file structure, you describe to the test data generator the form and content of each data field. INPUT-PRESSURE, for instance, might be a numeric field of two digits on each side of the decimal point with a range of 0 to 99.99. SCULP-TURE-NAME might be a 30-character field with effectively no constraints on content. The test data generator, given these field definitions and the others adequate to define the program input, would construct one or more test cases satisfying the specified definitions.

As checkout progresses, you elect to use a test coverage analyzer program to see if your automated test cases have adequately covered all program segments. The analyzer you choose has the additional capability of providing logic flow diagrams which show how particular program segments may be reached. Use of the analyzer shows that three segments remain untested. Via use of the flow diagrams, you deduce those values of input variables that will force the testing of the untested segments.

You have used two types of test case tools—the first, a test data generator, produced test cases but not comprehensively; and the second, an augmented test coverage analyzer, produced no test cases but provided in an automated fashion information which assisted you in completing the comprehensive test process.

REFERENCES

1.   "Generation, Processing and Application of Program Test Patterns," *Proceedings of the AIAA Computers in Aerospace Conference, 1977;* Miller.

Addresses the test case development aspect of a process the author calls "systematic testing." Defines a method for programmer insertion of test patterns which an automated test generator could use to deduce test cases. A test pattern is the set of I/O relationships that apply to a program segment.

2.   "On the Automated Generation of Program Test Data," *Proceedings of the 2nd International Conference on Software Engineering, 1976;* Ramamoorthy and Ho.

Discusses symbolic execution as a technique for the automated generation of a test case to exercise a specific program segment. Describes possible procedures for using a symbolic execution result and a prototype Fortran-oriented system called CASEGEN.

3.4.2.7   STANDARDIZED TESTING

The concept of *standardized testing* is analogous to that of generalized programming: Wouldn't it be nice if you didn't have to construct tests at all in order to wring out a new piece of software? Wouldn't it be nice if there were a library of available tests to draw from?

In most situations, that is not possible. If the requirements for the program you are writing are sufficiently unique to require it to be written at all, there probably is also a unique requirement for test case construction.

However, such is not always the case. Suppose that your problem is to implement a JOVIAL compiler for a new line of computers. There exists a standard set of test cases used for all such compilers, called the JOVIAL Compiler Validation System (JCVS), which can be used virtually unchanged to comprehensively test your compiler when it is complete.

Standardized testing, then, is the process of using a set of applicable generalized test cases (developed independent of a particular project) to test software.

An analogous situation is the benchmark test. A *benchmark* is a standardized test designed to exercise one or more competitive systems in order to evaluate them. Whereas the goal of standardized testing is normally to assist in program debugging and, perhaps, to use as a basis for sanctioning or certifying the program as a correct and acceptable implementation, the goal of the benchmark is to evaluate, with an implied decision regarding program usage at stake.

State of the Art in Standardized Testing

Rare are the situations where standardized testing is applicable. When it is, however, the concept is extremely valuable.

There are only a few standardized tests around. In addition to the previously mentioned JCVS test, there is also a standardized COBOL compiler validation system, and another for Fortran, both available from the National Technical Information Service. As will be seen in the references, work has also been done on ALGOL compiler and Fortran library standardized tests. For application programs per se, there are very few such tests.

Cost of Standardized Testing

Construction of a standardized test system is expensive, but the cost is totally application-dependent. With usage, the construction cost can fairly quickly be amortized. Users of standardized tests, of course, have significant cost reduction due to the avoidance of the need to construct their own tests.

Examples of Standardized Testing

The standardized tests for the JOVIAL compiler consist of several thousand JOVIAL statements which are compiled and executed to test any new compiler system. The statements are chosen to span the spectrum of allowable inputs (in this case, JOVIAL statements). Machine-dependent parameters (e.g., word length, number of bits per character) are isolated and flagged for ease of change for a test on a new computer system. The result of each portion of the test (in this case, execution of one or more JOVIAL statements) is tested by a JOVIAL conditional statement in order to make the tests self-checking.

To generalize this concept, forgetting for the moment that a JOVIAL compiler is being tested, the standardized test contains (1) a comprehensive set of inputs, (2) a simple mechanism for making the standardized test specific to a particular situation, and (3) a mechanism to simplify test result analysis. These concepts should characterize any standardized test.

138

REFERENCES

1. "The Navy Fortran Validation System," *Proceedings of the National Computer Conference, 1977;* Hoyt.

Describes the development and rationale for a Fortran compiler validator. Shows content of specific Fortran statement tests and discusses usage experience.

2. "The DoD COBOL Validation System," *Proceedings of the Fall Joint Computer Conference, 1972;* Baird.

Discusses the need for, history of, and implementation of a COBOL compiler standardized test system called CCVS (COBOL compiler validation system).

3. "Testing ALGOL 60 Compilers," *Software—Practice and Experience,* Apr.–June, 1976; Wickman and Jones.

Describes the process for constructing a set of ALGOL 60 compiler tests, discusses their effectiveness, and gives the result of their application to four compilers.

4. "Mathematical Software Testing Activities," *Program Test Methods,* Prentice-Hall, 1973; Ng.

Certification of mathematical software, such as Fortran libraries, is discussed. A variety of test methodologies are described, and favorable results are cited.

3.4.2.8   INTERACTIVE DEBUG

There are two distinct methods of approaching a computer for program test purposes; *batch* processing, where the programmer submits his job to the computer with the understanding that it will be placed in a queue to be run when the computer is ready for it, and *interactive* processing, where the programmer submits his job expecting instant and ongoing response from the computer. All the other information in Section 3 deals with techniques that are certainly applicable to the batch environment and perhaps to the interactive one as well; this paragraph deals with techniques and capabilities of the interactive system alone.

Interactive debug is the process of seeking and correcting errors in a computer program while communicating with the computer executing the program. Typically, the communication takes the form of monitoring program progress, inspecting intermediate values, inserting data corrections as needed, and in general controlling program execution.

So far in this discussion there has been no description of how the programmer might be enabled to communicate with his computer on the fly. There are two basic ways—one, via a timesharing system, in which a specially designed operating system allows a set of users at remote terminals to, in effect, share the computer's facilities simultaneously; and the other, via a hands-on-the-computer approach, in which the user sits at the computer's console, is its only user, and controls what it does. Obviously, these two methods are radically different from one another, even though they both result in the possibility of interactive debug.

State of the Art in Interactive Debug

A discussion of the state of the art in interactive debug must acknowledge the dichotomy between the timesharing approach and the hands-on approach.

Timesharing interactive debug exploded into prominence conceptually in the late 1960s, when it was hailed as one of the brilliant new concepts of computing. Because timesharing and interactive debug combine to effect a dramatic reduction in the time needed to debug a program (the programmer can accomplish in a short session on the terminal what would normally require several batch turnarounds, in many computing installations equated to several days), devotees of timesharing advocate total usage of the technology for program development efforts.

There are, however, some other considerations. For one, the programmer has less time between turnarounds for other work, such as documentation or working on another program, so that his productivity does not rise as dramatically as his debug time drops; and for another, the programmer may tend to make snap judgments on program revisions since they can be made "instantly," rather than sitting back and considering alternative revisions in a more leisurely and thoughtful environment.

Thus the timesharing state of the art is likely to be one of "choosing up sides"; either a computer installation emphasizes timesharing usage, or it has no timesharing capability at all. And the incidence of actual timesharing interactive debug capability is somewhat smaller than the total timesharing population, since interactive debug requires either language processors or debug support packages conditioned to allow programmer interaction during program execution.

Hands-on interactive debug is a totally different matter. In the early days of computing, before the advent of operating systems and computer operators, it was the only way to debug a program. It was quickly phased out once these "new" concepts came along in the late 1950s, since it was obviously a waste of computer time and programmer time to have the programmer's operationally unskilled hands at the controls. In recent years, however, with real-time computers and minicomputers and microcomputers becoming important components of the computing milieu, there has been a trend back toward hands-on debug. Interactive debug stand-alone packages (they require no operating system) are more and more frequently a part of the support software for such computers. It is interesting to speculate on whether this trend will phase out, as it did once before, in the 1950s.

Cost of Interactive Debug

The cost picture of interactive debug is mixed. Timesharing interactive debug entails major acquisition costs—a timesharing operating system, an interactive language processor, phone lines, and remote terminals. Ongoing costs are probably mildly more than batch systems.

Hands-on interactive debug, on the other hand, uses a bare-bones computer with only some sort of debug support software package. The clumsiness of the often-primitive tools may well make ongoing costs higher than batch operating systems, but this is difficult to measure.

Examples of Interactive Debug

Suppose that you have just walked up to your favorite timesharing terminal, logged on, done a little housekeeping of your files, and are now ready to make a debug run of your FOUNTAIN simulation program. You invoke a compiler with interactive debug capability, and sit back to monitor the results.

Owing to your source language debug preplanning, fairly soon your program begins printing a series of trace outputs, showing the values of several key variables as they change.

Then you notice it. One of the variables, output volume, is going sour—its values are clearly beyond tolerances. (Note that you have just performed the role of a human assertion checker.) Quickly, you push the attention key on your terminal to interrupt the execution of your program before it goes too far and obliterates the immediate evidence of the problem. Via the system's interactive debug capability, you probe through your program's data base, keying in the names of program variables and monitoring the responses as the system prints out the value of those variables. Narrowing the problem down, you see that one intermediate value in a complex calculation leading up to obtaining output volume is totally wrong. Referring to your program listing, you see that the arithmetic expression for that intermediate value is coded badly.

Using another function of the interactive debug system, you rewrite the erroneous expression and substitute the new correct source code for the old in your FOUNTAIN program. In the hopes of restarting the program from the point of interruption, you direct the interactive debug system to start up your program again at the point of the revised statement, rather than where you interrupted it.

The system returns control to your program, and off it goes again, executing and printing trace outputs. Your correction appears to have been a good one; the variable that had gone sour now looks reasonable, and you allow execution to proceed to completion.

You might well wonder how an interactive debug system allows this powerful capability. Many of them are *interpreters,* compilers that control the execution of a program as well as its compilation. Thus when you push attention, inspect variable values, change program statements, and request program resumption, you are communicating with the interpreter, acting as an interactive debug system, rather than your program. Many BASIC and APL language systems use this approach.

Other systems, such as the Fortran processor on the Computer Sciences Corp. Timesharing System (CSTS), use a normal compiler but have a layer of interactive debug control between the program and the operating system. CSTS has a Fortran-level program checkout facility (PCF) by means of which the user can perform services such as those discussed above, wherein PCF communicates with an internal system dictionary for the user's program produced by the compiler for execute-time use.

REFERENCES

1. "Debugging in a Time-sharing Environment," *Proceedings of the 1968 Fall Joint Computer Conference;* Bernstein and Owens.

Cites debugging aids as an area of little progress; proposes the "debugging support system" which system programmers could use to analyze tasks executing in a timesharing environment. A set of commands useful to the user of such a system is defined.

2. "A Production Environment Evaluation of Interactive Programming," U.S. Army Computer Systems Command Technical Documentary Report USACSC-AT-74-03, 1974; Reaser, Priesman, and Gill.

Describes an evaluation of interactive versus batch software development by the Army using COBOL programmers on the IBM 360 Timesharing Option (TSO). Programmer productivity and development cost were found to be significantly improved using timesharing. Tasks, experience levels, and methods of data collection are described.

3. "Timesharing vs. Batch Processing, The Experimental Evidence," *Proceedings of the 1968 Spring Joint Computer Conference;* Sackman.

Summarizes the pros and cons of timesharing usage, and the results of five experimental studies into the use of timesharing. Interpretation of study results shows (1) less expenditure of human time when programming in a timesharing environment, (2) more expenditure of computer time, and (3) programmer preference for timesharing.

3.4.2.9 INTENTIONAL FAILURE

Intentional failure is a process for honing the accuracy of, and measuring the thoroughness of, the debug process. It consists of deliberately introducing errors into a program, seeing how many are caught by those performing debug tasks, and using those results to establish confidence levels for the number of errors in the program and how long it will take to find them.

There is another way in which this process impacts software reliability. The existence of planted errors will, in some cases, motivate the error seeker to look harder.

State of the Art in Intentional Failure

Little use is known of the intentional failure concept in a software production environment. As the problem of software reliability comes more and more into focus as a serious concern, reliability methodologies from other fields are suggested for software. Some are more applicable than others. This methodology would appear to have little promise in the software field, chiefly because introducing intentional errors that are representative of the set of actual errors requires a better crystal ball than most technologists possess.

Cost of Intentional Failure

The cost of intentional failure is relatively inconsequential. However, a program-knowledgeable person who is not the error seeker must plant the intentional failure. Because of the feasibility problems with the methodology, it is difficult to be more specific about costs.

Examples of Intentional Failure

Suppose that you are just one of a team of programmers who all have knowledge of the internals of the FOUNTAIN simulation system. You decide to use intentional failure to help check it out. One of the programmers is selected to be excluded from the debug team and to be the error planter.

The programmer goes through the code, intentionally changing it in a variety of ways and places so that it will fail, recording each of the errors for later checkoff as they are found. He may, for example, change the initial value of a data variable; modify a loop-ending parameter; invert the order of calculation of two interdependent variables; remove a procedure formal parameter. He then sits back and waits for results.

The debug team proceeds in a normal manner to seek out errors. Each error is checked with the "planter" to see if it is one of his, in order to check it off properly. The progress in discovery of planted errors is monitored, and extrapolated results are given to management estimating the total number of errors remaining to be found, and the projected date of end of testing.

REFERENCES

1.   *Software Metrics,* pp. 26–49, Winthrop, 1977; Gilb.

Describes "debugging," the author's term for intentional failure—how to seed representative errors and what to do with the results. Discusses possible automation of the debugging concept.

3.4.2.10   FOREIGN DEBUG

One of the problems of program testing is that the person conducting the test is hardly a disinterested bystander. Having worked hard to design and/or implement his program, the programmer may have an ego investment in it or a myopia about it which precludes his wanting to or being able to find fault with it.

Foreing debug is an attempt to overcome that problem. It is the use of someone other than the original programmer to debug a program.

There are several interrelated concepts involved here. Peer code review, a static process for becoming familiar with and seeking errors in a program, is one of the concepts (it was discussed in Section 3.4.1.2). Product test, a management process for assigning responsibility to test case construction and execution to a disinterested group, is another of the concepts (it will be discussed in a subsequent section).

Foreign debug incorporates peer code review and product test and goes one step further—it not only assigns to a disinterested group responsibility for understanding and testing the program, but for fixing the errors so discovered as well.

State of the Art in Foreign Debug

Foreign debug is largely an experimental technique; it is not common practice in the production computing world. Its component parts, peer code review and product test, are more commonly used. The additional foreign debug step of having the surrogate programmer actually fix the problem seems somewhat counterproductive; the original programmer may never fully realize what he did wrong and thus miss a learning experience; and the surrogate may find it difficult to meld his programming philosophy and style with that of the original programmer. Additionally, the surrogate who is less familiar with the program may take longer to isolate and correct the error than the original programmer.

Sometimes foreign debug is necessary, however. When a program is received from another computing installation, or maintenance of a program changes hands, then there is no alternative to foreign debug.

Cost of Foreign Debug

Because of the added learning experiences necessary for the foreign debugger, this concept has a "getting-on-board cost," perhaps 20% over the normal test phase costs.

Examples of Foreign Debug

Suppose that you are assigned to foreign debug the FOUNTAIN program mentioned in an earlier section.

At the end of coding, you join a peer code review to become familiar with the workings of FOUNTAIN. Between review sessions, you read the documentation on the program, both its user manual and its maintenance manual.

As your learning progresses, you map out a debugging approach to the program and begin building test cases. When the review is complete, you append to the program any debug concepts you wish to use, such as source language debug statements and assertions, and begin the test.

As errors emerge in the testing process, it is your responsibility to fix them. This means modifying the program, and retesting. You may or may not consult with the original programmer in the process. But the total responsibility for debugging, and declaring the program ready for use, is yours.

REFERENCES

1. "An Exploratory Experiment with 'Foreign' Debugging of Programs," *Proceedings of the Symposium on Computer Software Engineering, 1976;* Musa.

    Describes a small experiment in the use of foreign debugging techniques, analyzing time consumed by debuggers, and benefits achieved. A number of value judgments relating to improved software techniques are presented. Concludes that the chief benefit of foreign debugging is as a mutual education and performance-feedback mechanism.

3.4.2.11   SYMBOLIC EXECUTION

All the testing methodologies described in this section deal with exercising a program on data selected to be similar to operational input data. *Symbolic execution,* a radically different concept, involves the algebraic execution of the symbolic version of a program upon symbolic input data. A special symbolic execution tool is required. The source program to be symbolically tested is fed into the tool, along with a set of input data classes. Each statement of the program is "executed" in normal go-time sequence, but the result of execution is the algebraic symbolic substitution into the expression in the statement of the input and any previously "computed" data.

Obviously, the result in a program of any size will be a dramatic increase in the complexity of expressions as program execution progresses. In addition, as conditional statements are encountered, the symbolic execution tool will likely find it impossible to determine which path should be taken. Therefore, some symbolic execution tools are built to interact with the programmer user, so that human decision making can steer the program in simplified and promising directions.

It is difficult to grasp the potential of a tool of this type. On the one hand, there is enormous promise to the symbolic test concept, since a single symbolic test case is equivalent to an infinite number of traditional numeric test cases. On the other hand, the complexity of the symbolic process may make that promise unreachable in a practical sense. In addition to the previously mentioned conditional statement problem, there is a serious problem in the symbolic execution domain involving subscript and pointer-type variables. They are essentially unserviceable, since the result of using such a variable negates the ability to develop a meaningful symbolic expression (e.g., what previously obtained expression does A[I] point to?). Until this problem is solved (if ever), symbolic execution cannot have broad usefulness. It may be useful in a local domain of a complex computational program, however, to help clarify the occurrence of a problem. In that sense, symbolic execution is a formalization and generalization of desk checking.

Symbolic execution may also be useful in proof-of-correctness techniques, by symbolically executing assertions to demonstrate correctness.

State of the Art in Symbolic Execution

Symbolic execution is still a research environment concept. Little usage has occurred in the production software environment. The difficulties in usage caused by such complications as subscript/pointer variables and conditional statements may well keep symbolic execution from having any broad practical value.

Cost of Symbolic Execution

There is no well-defined best approach to symbolic execution. The process can be done manually, as discussed in an industrial example later in this book. Or it can be done via an interactive processor, as described earlier in this section. The acquisition cost of a symbolic execution capability, then, may vary from zero to over $200,000, depending on method of approach.

Ongoing usage costs are equally difficult to quantify. Probably the tool will not be used unless there is a particularly complex mathematical portion of a program that is malfunctioning. Under those emergency circumstances, symbolic execution may well be cheaper than any other alternative, such as manual desk checking. Attempts to use symbolic execution on a broader scale would be more costly.

Examples of Symbolic Execution

Suppose a highly mathematical part of the FOUNTAIN system is not providing correct answers to the input data fed it. Visual inspection of both the code and the algorithm give you no clues as to the problem. Therefore, you elect to try symbolic execution. An interactive symbolic execution system is available on your company's timesharing computer.

You define a set of input data in algebraic terms. INPUT-FLOW-RATE, for instance, may be defined as the result of a quadratic equation; the gate BYPASS-VALVE may be defined as "even" (all even values represent "open"). These expressions, and the expressions of the algorithm itself in the form of the program's source code, are input to the symbolic executor. Using algebraic substitution, the tool proceeds through the algorithm code statement by statement, making appropriate substitutions from the preceding algebraic manipulations into the current one. The execution pauses after each statement, giving you the opportunity to inspect and mull over the results, and select (where necessary) the appropriate branch of a conditional statement. You can also guide the meaning of subscript and pointer variables, to the extent that you are able.

Watching the algorithm behave as symbolic execution proceeds, you spot an anomaly in the behavior. The simulated BYPASS-VALVE has become stuck shut; program conditions that should result in its opening have failed to do so. Upon further inspection, the error becomes apparent to you, and you correct it. A simple assignment statement opening the valve has been omitted from one program branch. Reexecuting the program symbolically, your FOUNTAIN flow now behaves properly.

REFERENCES

1. "Symbolic Execution and Program Testing," *Communications of the ACM,* July, 1976; King.

Defines symbolic execution as a middle ground between the extremes of testing and proving. Describes a symbolic execution tool called EFFIGY, being built by the author, which provides debug tools in an interactive environment for symbolic execution. Strengths and weaknesses are discussed, both of the concept and the specific tool.

2. "SELECT—A Formal System for Testing and Debugging Programs by Symbolic Execution," *1975 International Conference on Reliable Software;* Bayer, Elspas, and Levitt.

An experimental symbolic execution system, SELECT, is described. Examples of use are given, with limitations discussed. Other similar systems are mentioned.

3.4.2.12   MATHEMATICAL CHECKERS

Programs with a heavy mathematical flavor need special test tools. Not only is it difficult to determine whether a minor error in the second decimal place of a coded constant has been made, but it is also possible that because of such computing artifices as word length, even a correctly coded algorithm may behave improperly.

The previous paragraph on symbolic execution deals with this problem. So does the static technique of desk checking. This paragraph deals with two more mathematical reliability tools, the mathematical accuracy checker and the mathematical significance checker.

The *mathematical accuracy checker* is a process by which the accuracy of a computerized mathematical solution is evaluated. The accuracy checker accepts as input previously computed values (perhaps obtained by hand, perhaps via a simulator), the coded version of the equations to be solved, and does a parallel printout of computed results and input numbers, for manual inspection for differences.

The *mathematical significance checker* is a process by which the significance of a computerized mathematical solution may be monitored. A special processor—perhaps an interpreter for some sommonly used algorithmic language—keeps track of the significant digits or bits of accuracy in each equation as it is executed. The significance of each variable is also maintained in a symbol table or name list. As results are printed by the program, the significance of those results is also printed. At the conclusion of execution, the final significance (and value) of each variable may also be printed. Loss of significance due to roundoff, word length, or algorithmic ineptitude may thus be tracked by the user of the significance checker.

State of the Art in Mathematical Checkers

Neither of the mathematical checkers described herein is in common use. Desk checking, manual mathematical capabilities, and a certain amount of blind faith seem to be the state-of-the-art alternatives.

Cost of Mathematical Checkers

The acquisition cost of a mathematical checker is significant. Likely, it will require a special execute-time support package, perhaps embedded in an interpreter, to maintain the necessary results/significance data. This can cost up to $200,000 (at professional rates and industrial overheads).

Ongoing usage costs may also be high. The extra computing work necessary to track results or significance exacts a timing penalty. If the solution is use of an interpreter instead of a compiler, each test run may cost 20 to 30 times the comparable nonchecking figures.

Examples of Mathematical Checkers

As the result of painful past experience in the use of mathematically oriented programs, you are gunshy about the results of your nearly complete FOUNTAIN simulation program. You decide, based on the fortuitous in-house availability of a mathematical checker package, to subject your program to further analysis.

Adding to your good fortune, you have saved the computed results used to test out the mathematical aspects of your flow algorithm prior to putting it into code. Therefore, you prepare these results as input for the mathematical checker, turn on a significance option, and submit your job to the computer.

When the results come back, your suspicions are validated. The significance, you are gratified to see, is tolerable at each step of the process. However, miscoding of a sign on a simple assignment statement has led to a minor distortion of the final results.

You correct the error, resubmit the job, and now find both significance and accuracy acceptable. (Happily-ever-after stories appear in books in every field.)

REFERENCES

1. "Mathematical Software Testing Activities," *Program Test Methods,* Prentice-Hall, 1973; Ng.

Certification of mathematical software, such as Fortran libraries, is discussed. A variety of test methodologies are described and favorable results cited.

2. "A Method of Testing Programs for Data Sensitivity," *Program Test Methods,* Prentice-Hall, 1973; Bright and Cole.

"Significant digit arithmetic" is discussed as a means of tracking loss of significance in mathematical calculations. The Sig Pac system is described, and examples of use given. Comments are made about the economics of usage, and the suggestion is made that the future may see firmware implementation of significance analysis.

3. "SPLINTER—A PL/1 Interpreter Emphasizing Debugging Capability," *Computer Bulletin,* Sept., 1968; Glass.

In a discussion of a specific interpretive language processor, mathematical significance checking capabilities are described. Significance can be traced at each assignment statement or for specific variables, and can be dynamically turned on and off. A postmortem dump of all data variables also contains their significance.

3.4.3 Acceptance testing

For the most part, the preceding software reliability activities take place in the sanctity of the software development domain. The time must come, however, to show and tell the newly developed and checked out software to the user world outside. This exposure is usually conducted through the formality of the acceptance test.

An acceptance test is the checkout of software via a formally defined and conducted test in the presence of and requiring the approval of the software customer.

Acceptance testing typically takes place as part of the delivery and installation of the software at the customer's site (if the customer is the development organization, of course, this fact is of no consequence). The process will usually consist of an installation by the development team, conduct of the acceptance test, and, following approval of the test results, formal delivery.

Considerable thought has generally gone into the acceptance test well before it occurs. It may well have been defined by an acceptance test plan, and that document may have been reviewed as early as the software critical design review. As discussed in Section 4, the test plan probably describes the methodology of the test, the specific tests to be conducted, and the acceptance criteria for each test. Additionally, the test plan often contains a matrix relating all the requirements in the software specification to the test which shows achievement of that requirement.

Even if a formal test plan document does not exist, an alert customer will still insist on reviewing, in advance, test methodology, the manner of determining that the test performs satisfactorily, and the adequacy of the testing.

For small software projects, acceptance tests may end up being a simple and straightforward process. Even for large projects, the test should in general be straightforward, since presumably the development organization will have run the test previously at its own site. However, the realities of large software delivery seldom work out that way. Schedule constraints often force the developer into the acceptance test phase prior to the completion of in-house testing. As a result, the acceptance test is sometimes a traumatic process. Major software acceptance tests may frequently require 30 to 90 days of calendar time to complete, and failure of software to pass an acceptance test is not unheard of (the developers fall back to their lair to regroup, and the test is rescheduled for a time when the software has hopefully gotten well).

Not the least of the problems of the acceptance tester is the installation itself. Company A's Marketronics computer may behave rather differently from Company B's Marketronics, and an expert on the vagaries of the Marketronics job control language and operating system is a vital part of the installation team.

When available, standardized tests (see Section 3.4.2.7) are an important part of the acceptance test process.

State of the Art in Acceptance Testing

Early in the history of computing, there was no formal acceptance test. Often, the programmer would simply announce one day that the software was ready for use, hope for the best, and turn it over to the customer.

Usually, this process worked satisfactorily. When it did not, however, it was awful. The customer was at the mercy of the programmer's sense of responsibility, and if both it and the software were inadequate, the customer was in deep trouble.

The result of all of this was an increase in formalization of the acceptance process, culminating in the formal acceptance test. Especially in the Department of Defense domain, a formal test is usually now required for software products.

Cost of Acceptance Testing

There is cost, sometimes significant, to the acceptance test process. Test documentation, test generation, test conduct, and test result analysis each cost money. The amount of money is, of course, dependent on the application.

Example of Acceptance Testing

Your bookmaking program, defined in an earlier section, has finally achieved a sufficient state of readiness to be delivered to your customer. You catch a flight to Reno, along with a development teammate who is an expert on the customer's Quadranova computer operating system, and arrive at the customer's installation with a briefcase full of documents and a mag tape containing the program.

Although the customer is happy to see you, his computer is not. It is being used to capacity two shifts a day, and your testing is relegated to a time slot that you had forgotten existed on a 24-hour clock.

Bleary-eyed, you, your companion, your program, and your test cases arrive at the Quadranova at 2 A.M. The first night is spent wrestling with system control cards unique to the customer's installation. At last, your program takes hold and runs. Your companion catches a plane home.

On subsequent nights (the customer is generous enough to let you work first shift on weekends), you run a set of tests, then meet a member of the customer's technical team to review the night's results at 8 o'clock the next morning. The customer, fresh and alert, runs mental circles around your off-hours-tired brain, but he also, one by one, signs off as accepted the tests you have been running.

The blackjack test, in spite of all your previous effort, still has a bug related to the value of the ace of spades. You correct the bug the following night, rerun the test, and that result, too, is signed off.

After so long away from home, working undesirable hours in an environment your mother would find difficult to understand, you are happy to climb aboard a plane a week and a half later, an approved acceptance test report in your briefcase, and head home.

REFERENCES

1.   "Implementing a Software Quality Assurance Program for the Viking Lander Flight Software," *Transactions of the Software '77 Conference;* Prudhomme.

Describes the Viking spacecraft and its mission to explore Mars. Gives a detailed description of the verification/validation testing process, the facilities required to conduct the tests, and the sequence and content of the tests.

2.   "The Right Program—for the Wrong Problem," *The Universal Elixir and Other Computing Projects Which Failed,* Computing Trends, 1977; Glass.

A computing "horror story" about a project that passed all development tests and irrevocably failed its acceptance test.

3.5   MAINTENANCE TECHNIQUES

It is unfortunate but true that software implementation and testing do not conclude the software reliability process. Some elusive software errors invariably slip through the mesh set up to screen them out and must be dealt with "in the field." *Maintenance* is the term used for all such postcheckout reliability activity; it also includes the implementation of approved software revisions. Significant cost, and therefore significant importance, is attached to the maintenance process. But because of its lack of glamor, little research and tool development has been done in this area.

If reliability is the neglected urchin of computing, maintenance is its companion. Virtually no studies exist of ways of improving the software maintenance process. The literature is nearly vacuous; only the popular periodicals, especially those in the commercial data processing field, tend to deal with the subject at all. Researchers apparently avoid the matter entirely.

There is the rumble of distant drums on the software maintenance horizon, however. Government and especially military circles, which recently have shown intense concern for software reliability, resulting in the funneling of a great quantity of research dollars into that arena, are just beginning to notice the neglect of maintenance.

As well they might. Almost every study that attempts to quantize the cost of software maintenance comes up with ball park figures of 50% of total software life-cycle costs. Even the most conservative drop only to 40%; and there are some figures at the 80% level. Whatever the facts actually are, the conclusion is apparent—for all its lack of glamor, software maintenance is a field of significant implications.

There are some industry as well as academic reasons for the neglect. Maintenance, more than most other phases of the software life cycle, is not well understood. Managers, who might otherwise be the first ones to call for some help, tend to be awed by the mysterious manipulations of the maintainer who deals with the computer at its most intimate levels. More significantly, the status of maintenance activities apparently appears from a management point of view to be largely satisfactory. Managers tend to see software maintenance as more important than development, and maintenance productivity as not a problem, according to one survey of largely COBOL-oriented installations. Thus, there is little motivation to seek assistance in this area.

The term "maintenance" itself may be a misnomer. It tends to conjure up the picture of a Maytag repairman, overall-clad, keeping a 1950s-style washing machine running well beyond its obsolescence.

But, in fact, according to the survey mentioned previously, an extremely high percentage of software maintenance activity is not repair-oriented but involves enhancements! Thus, maintenance is really a shrouded kind of development activity, a kind of professional in overall clothing. (The study showed that 60% of maintenance activity was "perfective"—customer- and programmer-defined improvements to the program; 18% was "adaptive"—accommodation to changes in external factors such as data base formats or hardware or system software; and only 17% was "corrective"—fixes; the remaining 5% was the ever-popular "other.")

The manning of maintenance activities is a problem all its own. Most programmers tend to scorn it as uncreative. Even those who participate in it tend to recommend an "R and R" philosophy—rest and rehabilitation time on a tropical software development project after a fixed period of banishment to the Siberia of maintenance. Only a few actually enjoy maintenance. Usually, the unsuspecting newcomer is assigned to its depths.

The personality trait requirements on programmers who maintain are probably more severe than on other phases of the software life cycle. For one thing, in spite of all the attempts to standardize software development methodology, most programs have an underlying and unique development-programmer-introduced philosophy. It may be a good philosophy, or it may be a bad philosophy. It may be well understood by the programmer who created it, but more likely it is not. But if it cannot be adapted to by the programmer who becomes responsible for the program's maintenance, the program is doomed to die. Many more programs have been discarded and rewritten by maintainers who "didn't like" (couldn't adjust to) them than there are truly "bad" programs. Meshing of philosophies, and selection of adaptable programmers, is a not-well-understood requirement which should be imposed on the software maintenance manager.

The potential payoffs of effective software maintenance are large. In addition to the already discussed dollar factor, it should be kept in mind that the maintenance programmer is the most important kind of customer relations support the manager has. At the very least, the maintainer establishes the technical quality image that the customer will react to. And if the maintainer not only changes software but negotiates those changes with the customer, he personifies the human (as well as the technical) interface of the installation to its customer.

What a mixed picture, then, software maintenance brings into focus. Neglected by researchers. Scorned by programmers. Consumer of large amounts of dollars. Bread and butter of managers. Lifeline of customers. No wonder the subject of software maintenance will become increasingly important in the next few years of computing!

REFERENCES

1. "Characteristics of Application Software Maintenance," UCLA Graduate School of Management, 1976; Lientz, Swanson, and Tompkins.

Surveys 69 computing installations to identify the characteristics of software maintenance. Responsible for the data cited above. Studies largely COBOL-oriented environments with high ongoing maintenance needs.

2. "Software Engineering," *IEEE Transactions on Computers,* Dec., 1976; Boehm.

Defines software engineering and constituent parts. Discusses costs and trends. Section VII, Software Maintenance, says that maintenance accounts for about 70% of the cost of software and is a "highly neglected activity."

3. "A Study of Fundamental Factors Underlying Software Maintenance Problems," ESD-TR-72-121, Vol. 11; 1971.

A series of interviews with programmers on maintenance-relevant subjects. Also contains maintenance programmer diaries and case study reports.

3.5.1 Preventive maintenance

The best kind of maintenance is, of course, no maintenance at all. In the state-of-the-art unlikely event that the software is done right the first time, then at least the corrective and perhaps even the adaptive and perfective changes will not need to be made. "Doing it right the first time" means employing much of the reliability technology of the preceding sections of this book, and some additional blind luck as well.

But preventive maintenance is more than just the elimination of the need for maintenance. Preventive maintenance is also the use of techniques to make maintenance more comfortable, easier, and safer. Some of those techniques are enumerated below:

1. *Modularity.* A modular program is much more maintainable. Particularly if the Parnas philosophy on module selection is employed (see Section 3.3.2), changes will be isolated to a few modules rather than having scattered impact throughout the program.
2. *Parameterization.* Apparently constant parameters should be named and referenced by name throughout the program. Then if the "constant" is changed, only the definition need be changed, not each instance of it. This is especially true of capacity or limit constants.
3. *Prevention of self-destruction.* Overflow of a data table should be tested for, diagnosed, and reported to the user with appropriate recovery action. Too many programs blow up in mysterious ways when an "unexceedable" capacity is exceeded.
4. *Data structuring.* Use a language that provides for the definition of non-word-oriented data at declaration time, rather than at each instance of usage. Then when the structure of that data is changed, only its declaration, not each reference, needs to be changed. (Subordinate recommentation—avoid using Fortran!)
5. *Program structuring.* Avoid use of intertwined control constructs. Use IF-THEN-ELSE, BEGIN-END, with a readable indentation system. The realm of influence of a segment of code will be visually obvious; and so will the impact of its change.
6. *Margins.* Leave room in the program for you to have been wrong. Do not consume all the computer's memory or other resources. Select limits larger than reasonable. When changes are required, have a place to accommodate them.
7. *Standards and practices.* Seek to define and establish good practices. The peer code review is a good way of making

programmers aware of, and spreading the gospel of, good programming practices. Use naming conventions that reflect both the meaning and the structure of data or program modules. Maintain listings in alphabetic order by module name. Standards and good practices make a program more readable, less individual-philosophy-dependent.

8. *Documentation.* The most dependable source of maintenance information is the listing. Annotate it heavily with comments. Define a specific commentary standard. Include linkage requirements for all callable modules. Additionally, provide maintenance manual or project workbook documentation. Stress overview, philosophic, and historic information of value to the maintainer. Include pointers to the listing for detailed information. And *keep it current* as changes occur.

REFERENCES

1.   "Software Acquisition Management Guidebook, Software Maintenance Volume," System Development Corp. TM-5772/004/02, Nov., 1977; Stanfield and Skrukrud.

Describes preventive maintenance techniques throughout the software life cycle. Specifically directed toward DoD-procured software, but applies to all. Provides ideas and checklists for maintenance-oriented software review. Summarizes DoD regulations, specifications, and standards relevant to software maintenance.

2.   "Research Toward Ways of Improving Software Maintenance," ESD-TR-73-125, 1973; Overton, Colin, and Tillman.

Describes an experiment in which software maintenance activities were measured. Contains many quotes from maintenance programmers. Stresses the structure ("conceptual groupings") of the software. Defines specific maintainability techniques and a maintainability checklist. Discusses use of a graphics terminal to support maintenance.

3.   "Program Standards Help Software Maintainability," *1978 Proceedings of the Annual Reliability and Maintainability Symposium;* White.

Evaluates the impact of software standards on maintainability. Concludes that modularity, structured coding, and in-line commentary have merit.

3.5.2 Change review

Just as there is a review process for software development, so, too, is there review of maintenance. Change review includes not only a decision-making process on what changes to make and when to make them, but also tracking the background information necessary to those decisions.

Change review, then, may be considered a multifaceted process. Records should be kept of all software error reports, software change requests, and their status. Status will include date of origination, priority assigned to the change, and estimated completion date. The records themselves should be reviewed to determine whether maintenance activities are keeping up with change origination and thus whether manning is adequate, and to make sure that no change falls through the crack and is forgotten until some potentially embarrassing point in the future (see Section 3.5.4).

Change review also includes the process of deciding whether a change is appropriate and, if so, what priority to assign to it. Such a decision process must be both dependable and responsive; provision must be made for consideration of emergency changes, for example.

Usually, maintenance is an ongoing or "level-of-effort" activity. One or several programmers are assigned to maintain one or several pieces of software on a continuing basis, perhaps even interspersed with other development activities. Changes are scheduled dependent on both their importance and maintenance programmers availability. However, some computing installations with a heavy production-run orientation are using the concept of "scheduled maintenance"— changes are aggregated until a date defined in advance independent of the changes, and then all are put in at once. This technique will minimize the frequency of perturbances in the stability of the production program.

REFERENCES

1. "Maintenance of the Computer Sciences Teleprocessing System," *Proceedings of the International Conference on Reliable Software, 1975;* Bucher.

Describes maintenance activities on a specific project. Stresses management of maintenance. Shows the role of the "Change Advisory Board" and "System Evolution Conference." Discusses change records, and testing techniques.

2.   "Scheduled Maintenance of Applications Software," *Datamation,* May, 1973; Lindhorst.

Advocates scheduled maintenance. Discusses its benefits and problems.

3.   "E-3A Software Maintenance," *Proceedings of the AIAA Conference on Computers in Aerospace, 1977;* Fox.

Describes maintenance activities on a DoD command and control project. Discusses the E-3A project itself, the management structure for software maintenance, and the activities involved (including change reporting).

4.   "Viking Software Data," RADC-TR-77-168, "Software Change Request/Impact Summary," pp. 222–228, 1977.

A frank discussion of the problems of change review on the Viking project. Includes forms and methodologies used.

3.5.3   Regression testing

Preventive maintenance is generally a before-the-fact kind of thing. But regression testing is a "head-em-off-at-the-pass" form of maintenance that occurs in the midst of the change activity.

Regression testing is a method of detecting errors in changes, or spawned by changes, made during software maintenance. It consists of the use of a well-defined set of tests, applied to the new release-ready version of the software after one or more changes have been made. The purpose of these tests is to ensure that the change has been correctly made, that the problem to be corrected has indeed "gone away," and that no other part of the software has been spoiled by the change.

These are not idle concerns. Change-caused errors are a chronic problem of software maintenance. All too frequently a new software release may correct X problems but cause Y new ones. The impact on the user, who cries "This used to work, why doesn't it now?" can be devastating, and software credibility can be destroyed if Y is large.

Fortunately, there are techniques for making good regression tests. First of all, if acceptance testing was performed, those tests should form the nucleus of the regression tests. But the regression tests should also be a dynamic thing. As errors are found and corrected, tests specific to those changes should be run and also added to the regression test set. Particularly if the software is fragile or vulnerable in certain areas, tests of those areas should be included.

Just as important as the breadth of the tests is their design. Since they are run frequently, regression tests should be self-checking. That is, not only should they contain data to detect errors, but processes designed to isolate, identify, and report what those errors are. The importance of this is that, since the regression test is hopefully large, a reduction in the human time necessary to review the results is directly related to the motivation to run the test. One method of self-checking results is the use of a correct output file and a file comparator program to detect differences between it and test results.

Regression tests should also be self-documenting. The test itself should contain a description of what it tests, how it tests it, and what to do in the event of failure. Again, reduction of maintainer review and reaction time is the goal.

REFERENCES

1.   "Automatic Software Test Drivers," *Computer,* Apr., 1978; Panzl.

Discusses regression testing ("under present technology, effective regression testing is seldom possible") in the context of an automatic system for producing and retaining test procedures.

2.   "Maintenance of the Computer Sciences Teleprocessing System," *Proceedings of the International Conference on Reliable Software, 1975;* Bucher.

Describes maintenance methodology, especially managerial, on a specific project. Discusses design and goals of tests. Examples are shown.

3.   "MAIDS Study—Program Testing and Diagnosis Technology," Letter Report N7000-6-73, 1973; Goodenough and Eanes.

Discusses the inadequacy of testing and the importance of early detection of design errors. Includes regression testing in a general discussion of testing strategies.

3.5.4   Error reporting

Software errors are a diverse and difficult lot. They range from the trivial (e.g., syntactic errors resulting from misuse of a language, detected by the language processor) to the complex (e.g., a logic error resulting only from the execution of a peculiar combination of program logic paths, detectable only by constructing an input case which forces the execution of that combination).

Software errors emerge from all phases of the software life cycle. Recent data tend to show a preponderance of errors resulting from the design phase; this may be because design is really the most error-prone phase of the life cycle, or it may be because most error reporting systems do not begin tracking errors until the software is placed under configuration control, a point in the cycle when many coding errors have been detected and corrected. Be that as it may, the source of errors has as diverse and difficult a picture as their nature.

Because software errors are a serious problem, a software error reporting system is often necessary. Because of the diversity of errors, their sources, and their ways of detection, central control of that error reporting system is also often necessary.

The purpose of an error reporting system is:

1. To ensure that errors are corrected, not forgotten.
2. To ensure that all error corrections are approved before changes are made.
3. To enable the measuring of error correction progress.
4. To provide feedback to the user on error status.
5. To prioritize the order in which errors are corrected.

It is important to report and track software problems. It is also important to know when to track, and for how long.

Typically, in the software life cycle, a great amount of error detection will occur before a formal tracking system is necessary. Errors discovered in the analysis and design phases, for example, are generally not tracked, since they are usually corrected in the emerging specification and design as they are discovered. Even during the code and checkout phase, errors usually are not tracked because they are too numerous and because the time to fix is often less than the time to report. It is after a software product begins acceptance testing, or is released to the customer, or begins system integration (preferably, whichever comes first) that a formal tracking system becomes necessary.

All errors reported under the error reporting system should be recorded on some sort of *Software Problem Report* (SPR) form.

The SPR becomes the primary vehicle for tracking problems. A sample SPR form is shown in Figure 3.8. The process for processing this form is discussed in the succeeding paragraphs of this section. An illustration of a possible SPR processing flow, showing organizational responsibilities as well as actions, is given in Figure 3.9.

Problem Report Processing

Whenever a software problem is discovered after the tracking system is initiated, an SPR must be filled out and a number assigned it. The SPR should clearly state the problem symptoms, and be accompanied by physical evidence of the existence of the problem and sufficient information to allow its re-creation.

Types of errors that are reportable include:

1. Software malfunction (self-contained or interfacing).
2. Documentation error.
3. Software inefficiency.
4. Test case/procedure error.

A priority for correction of the error should be established. The priority should take into account the generality of the problem (Is it disabling? Will it impact other usage?), the ability to work around it, the degree to which the originator himself is stopped by the occurrence, and the relative importance of the originator's work. The priority should be noted prominently on the SPR form.

The SPR, once filled out, should be given to the responsible software organization.

The software maintainer should briefly examine the SPR to see if it may impact a program portion he is already working on, and to determine its priority. The SPR should then be filed, pending its emerging to be worked in priority sequence.

When the SPR comes up for work, an analysis of the problem and determination of a probable correction is made. The result of this analysis is noted on the SPR form. The nature of the correction is then submitted to the change review process, if any (see Section 3.5.2).

Once change approval is received (if necessary), the software correction is coded and inserted into the program. The updated code,

SOFTWARE PROBLEM REPORT

Problem Report No. _____

Project Name _____ Computer/Lab Utilized _____ Program _____

| Problem Discovery | Name of finder _____ Date _____ |

Method of detection □ Development test | Tools used to detect □ Dump (terminal) □ Simulation
□ Usage   □ Integration test | □ None   □ Dump (dynamic) □ Assertion
□ Inspection/Analysis □ Acceptance test | □ Design review   □ HOL Debug   □ Proof
                                        | □ Peer review   □ Analyzer   □ Other

Description of symptoms _____

_____

Configuration level _____

Correction importance/need date _____

Authorizing Signature _____ Orgn. _____ Date _____

| Problem Analysis | Name of analyst _____ Start date _____ End date _____ |

Findings _____

Resources expended: person _____ computer _____

Estimated resources to correct: person _____ computer _____

| Problem Correction | Name of programer _____ Start date _____ End date _____ |

Description of Correction _____

_____

Components changed and configuration level _____

Resources expended: person _____ computer _____

Problem category -
□ Job control language   □ Design error - omitted logic   □ Documentation
□ Operational Interface   □ Design error - faulty logic   □ Other
□ Coding error - data declaration   □ Testing
□ Coding error - executable instruction □ Configuration management

Final Authorizing Signature _____ Orgn. _____ Date _____

Figure 3.8 Suggested Software Problem Report Form

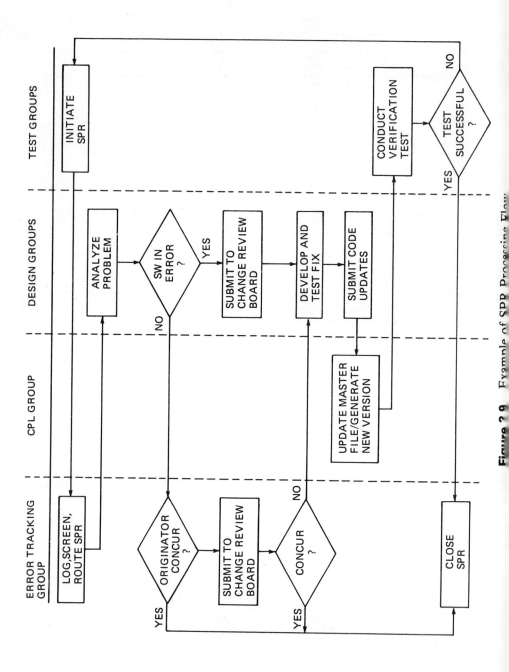

Figure 2.9 Example of SPR Processing Flow

perhaps including corrections to one or more other problems, is then executed against the specific test situations on which it failed. If it passes that test, the corrected software is then executed against a regression test (see Section 3.5.3), to ensure that no problems have been created by the correction. If any of these tests fail, the correction must be redesigned and recoded and retested. If all tests succeed, the software is ready to be considered for release to its previous environment (acceptance test, usage, . . .).

Problem Status Report

Developers, users, and managers need to be kept aware of the status of specific problems as well as the general status of the software. To this end, a problem status report is needed.

The problem status report originates from the SPR file. It should cover at least the following, preferably by priority:

1. New problems reported, their nature, and their probable disposition.
2. Old open problems, their nature, and their probable correction date.
3. Problems closed since the last report, their nature, and the disposition.
4. Trends data. A graph showing the history of the count of open SPRs and the history of problem reporting frequency.

Via the problem status report, it should be possible to look up the status of any given problem, check to see if a problem you have encountered may already be on the list, and grasp the overall progress in removing errors from the software.

REFERENCES

1. "Error Data Collection in Software Systems," "Computer Software Reliability, Many State Markov Modeling Techniques," RADC-TR-169, 1975; Trivedi and Shooman.

Discusses the process of error reporting in the context of reliability modeling studies. Suggests improvements in current reporting techniques to assist the error modeler.

2.   "The Dimensions of Maintenance," *Proceedings of the 2nd International Conference on Software Engineering, 1976;* Swanson.

Proposes to define theoretical bases of software maintenance. Defines corrective, adaptive, and perfective maintenance. Suggests contents of a maintenance data base, and measure of maintenance performance. Recommends further research into the subject.

3.5.5   Other maintenance techniques

The task of maintaining a significant piece of software is usually performed without benefit of specifically designed reliability tools, with the possible exception of the regression test.

However, any tool or technique that assists the maintainer and allows him to minimize the task of program revision probably assists the reliability of the product as well.

In that spirit, brief descriptions of the applicability of three additional maintenance tools are given here. Cross-reference listings, calling levels analysis, and procedure parameter references listings may be implemented manually, but automated tools in general are the only practical way to obtain the required information with the required reliability.

Cross-reference listings traditionally are produced by compilers at the individual program level, showing each name in the program, where it is defined, and where it is referenced. Much less commonly, they may be produced by a linkage editor showing the same information for large systems of programs, treating the names in the system-wide date base and external procedures in a similar manner. They are extremely valuable tools in maintenance for ensuring that, if one reference to a name is changed, all references are analogously changed. Additionally, a system-wide automated cross-reference tool can automatically extract from a program such information as a matrix or list of procedures referencing or referenced by another procedure, sometimes required in programming documentation.

Calling levels analysis helps clarify the interrelationships between subprograms, producing a listing of procedures, what they call, and how those calls are dynamically nested (as the program executes). Calling levels analysis is useful for a high-level understanding of subprogram relationships, and it is also useful in identifying inadvertent recursion or other strange program behavior.

Procedure parameter reference listings are of further value in subprogram interrelationships. Using this technique, all calls to a subprogram are listed in order of parameter reference, showing the point of call of each. This kind of listing can supplement a cross-reference list for frequently referenced subprograms, particularly those whose usage may be distinguished by specific parameters. If a common diagnostic routine is used in a program, with one parameter being the diagnostic message or number, for example, then finding where a particular diagnostic is produced would be easy via such a list.

3.6   TECHNOLOGICAL TOOL AND TECHNIQUE SELECTION

It has been stated elsewhere in this guidebook that reliability has historically been the neglected child of computing. After plowing through the previous several sections, you may be beginning to wonder about the accuracy of that assessment. Page after page has described a plethora of products available. "So where's the problem?" you may be wondering.

There are a couple of problems. Reliability technology is still a software Johnny-Come-Lately. Many of the tools and techniques exist largely as gleams in the eye of researchers or are still experimental in nature, and reliability technology is fragmented. The loose structure of tools presented here is an accurate structural view of the emerging cornucopia of reliability technique; the user must poke around in the spilled-out contents to put together a package of software methodology for his own use.

Probably most important, reliability is costly. Having ad hoc'ed our way to relatively reliable software for years, we in the business of building software—and our funding sources—are reluctant to spread out significant amounts of money to achieve improved software reliability by some difficult-to-predict amount.

The process of putting together a software reliability package for a specific project will be dealt with in Section 5. It is the purpose of this section to discuss ways of selecting and evaluating tools, rather than which ones to select. The organization of the preceding sections is intended to be a help in that regard, in that the choices are grouped by phase of software development. But once you have decided to use a test coverage analyzer, for example, how do you go about choosing one? getting one? trying it out?

3.6.1   Selection methods

The set of steps leading to tool acquisiton should include surveying existing tools, a make-or-buy decision, comparison of candidates, and a trial application of the leading candidate. These steps are dealt with in more detail in what follows.

Survey Existing Tools

Suppose you have determined that you can have the strongest impact on software reliability at your installation by strengthening testing support. Suppose further that after analysis of that section of this guidebook, you would like to acquire a test coverage analyzer.

For your first exposure to a more in-depth understanding of analyzers, you pursue the references at the end of that section. Each of those references contains additional references. With adequate library support, you can be a nouveau riche expert in analyzers in less than a month.

From that exposure, you begin to understand who the experts are in the field of analyzers, where they work, and what their products (if any) are. Armed with the knowledge that you are both a customer and a colleague, call them up. Most experts are happy to share additional knowledge with anyone interested enough to have gotten an in-depth speaking knowledge of a technology area. In addition, they will be able to name available products, discuss implementation techniques, and point you to additional contacts.

As you move through your contacts, construct a matrix of available products—what the tool is, what it does (and does not do), who the contact is for further information, what language and computer it supports, how much it costs, what resources it requires, what documentation comes with it, and any other details to both help in the selection process and prevent you from acquiring something worthless.

At the conclusion of this process, you have a fairly complete listing of existing and available tools in your category of interest. You also understand a good deal more about analyzers and are better armed to make a competent selection. Now write a book on it.

Make-or-Buy Decision

Procurement people have a favorite term for the decision process in which a product is either to be built within the company or purchased outside. The process is called a *make-or-buy decision.* Your next action in the process of selecting an analyzer is to make one of those decisions.

The key parameters in your make-or-buy decision are:

1. The availability of a tool for the language and computer you have.
2. The portability of a tool to your computer.
3. The cost of such a tool.
4. The talent in your shop for building such a tool.

If you do not have that information, make the appropriate contacts to obtain it.

Typically, if a product is appropriately available, it will be cheaper than building your own, no matter what the cost (within reason). If the tool must be made operational on your computer, it may or may not be cheaper to buy than to build. If no talent is available in your shop, it will be cheaper to buy (or to do without).

In finalizing your make-or-buy decision, do not forget that there are costs of procurement over and above the off-the-shelf cost of the product. They include such things as evaluation costs, acceptance test costs, and (if the product is to be *built* by an outside firm) progress monitoring costs. These must be added to the purchase cost in contrasting with the "make" cost.

Comparison of Candidates

If your make-or-buy decision was "make," you are embarked on a new course, one to which this section of the guidebook is not relevant. But if you decided to buy, you may be faced with the problem of choosing among more than one candidate.

Studying product specifications is the first and most obvious step toward making such a choice. Evaluating the talent and stability of the company that produced it (or maintains it or both) is a not-so-obvious second step. Performing benchmark runs with live data at the company's (or your own) site is the third step. Scoring the results of this process and selecting a winner is the fourth (and last).

This cursory look at the comparison process should be taken as a challenge to pursue the matter further. A great deal has been written on the subject, and it is beyond the scope of this guidebook. The references at the end of this section give much more in-depth information about the selection process.

Trial Application

Once you have picked and procured a winner, step gingerly into the sea of usage. Rather than sign up a large project for total commitment to the tool, pick a small project or piece of a project as a pilot application. Try it out in that environment, to better understand its strengths and weaknesses. Gather data to quantize usage costs and benefits, to better enable you to describe the tool to subsequent users. Discover product faults and report them to the maintainers for repair. Be sure that your understanding of what the tool is good for matches reality in your shop's environment.

REFERENCES

1.   "Automated Tools for Software Quality Control," *Transactions of the Software '77 Conference;* Norum and Miller.

Categorizes, lists, and describes over 40 automated software reliability tools. Names products and discusses availability.

2.   "Cost-Benefit Analysis in Information Systems Development and Operation," *ACM Computing Surveys,* Mar., 1978; King and Schrems.

Defines and describes the evaluation of computing concepts by measuring their cost and value. The technique is illustrated and the realities of its frequent political misuse are dealt with.

3.   *Analysis, Design and Selection of Computer Systems,* College Readings, Inc., 1972; Joslin.

A compendium of readings on the subject of computer systems acquisition. Includes "Shopping for Commercial Software," "Systematic Techniques for Computer Evaluation and Selection," "Get the Computer System You Want," and "Contract Caveats."

3.6.2   A case study

The process that has just been described has frequently been used, and continues to be used, for software tool selection. To reinforce the description of the technique, the following case study is presented.

Company A, aware that software reliability was becoming increasingly important to its customers, decided to evaluate the available reliability tools and select one for further investigation. Knowing that testing was the traditional corporate focus of reliability efforts, Company A technologists elected to supplement testing technology rather than begin a totally new methodology. Evolution, they knew, was easier to sell politically than revolution.

The technologists participating in the selection process were members of a group called software quality control. Organizationally, they were separate from any particular software project; their responsibility lay in an overview of all software projects and the provision of general-purpose tools.

The general-purpose tool they elected to evaluate was the test coverage analyzer. Surveying the then-available field of analyzers, they came up with the following list:

1. National Bureau of Standards (NBS) Fortran Analyzer. Originally implemented on Univac 1108, converted to several other computers.
2. McDonnell-Douglas Program Evaluator and Test (PET). Implemented on CDC 6600 series for the Fortran language, converted to several other computers.
3. General Research Corp. RXVP and JAVS (Automated Validation System). Implemented on CDC 6000 for Fortran (RXVP) and CDC and Honeywell 6000 for JOVIAL J3 (JAVS). JAVS development was funded by the Air Force via RADC (Rome Air Development Center).

4. TRW Product Assurance Confidence Tester (PACE). Implemented on CDC 6000 series, IBM 360, and Univac 1108 for Fortran.

The cost figures in this comparison told a decisive story. The NBS analyzer was in the public domain and available at no cost. With no further fanfare, it was selected and obtained from NBS.

However, the NBS analyzer serviced only Fortran. Company A had a high commitment to a customer that used the JOVIAL language. The only JOVIAL analyzer on the list, JAVS, was not available at that point, as it was undergoing an extended acceptance test process. As a result, the decision was made to implement a JOVIAL analyzer in-house and conduct an experiment using both tools. For several reasons, including reduced implementation cost and reduced user resource impact, a coarse-grain JOVIAL analyzer was implemented.

While the acquisiton and construction of the analyzers was in process, contact was made with a Company A software project to obtain agreement on an experiment environment. The A3 project decided to cooperate, and selected a few programs to be used as the basis for the experiment.

Overall goals of the experiment were (1) to determine viability of the use of the tool in a typical project environment, (2) to better evaluate resource impacts of tool usage (computer time and space, people time), (3) to familiarize project personnel with the tool, and (4) to provide test coverage metrics for project personnel.

The NBS was used on two A3 ground support software programs and on itself. The JOVIAL tool was used on a component of the A3 JOVIAL compiler, and on itself. (Each of the tools was coded in the language it analyzed.)

The two programs on which the NBS analyzer was used (besides itself) were (1) a message generator program, which consisted of about 45 subprograms, one of which was instrumented (the most important one); and (2) a configuration traceability program, all of which was instrumented.

The procedure on which the JOVIAL analyzer was used was the compool resolution portion of the compiler for the JOVIAL language.

None of the instrumented programs or subprograms could be considered major software systems; each was equivalent to a small, or small to medium, software development. The experiment was treated as a pilot rather than as a full-blown effort.

Results of the experiment are shown here as an example of the type of evaluation that such an experiment could show.

Fortran Analyzer Experiment Results

Each of the Fortran test programs was instrumented and executed. Ongoing efforts were then made, as described below, to iterate on the execution and resultant findings.

One of the major goals of the experiment was to determine the viability of using an analyzer in a typical project environment where there is significant schedule pressure on individual participants. The following findings were made:

1. Progress in using the analyzer was slow. This was primarily due to the low-priority nature of the experiment, not to the analyzer itself. A number of job control language and related operating system dependent user errors also slowed progress. None of these factors was considered significant with respect to analyzer evaluation.

2. Operational problems were encountered by both project users. One job ran extremely inefficiently when instrumented, and as a result several runs were aborted for exceeding computer time requests. In addition, one facet of input control information was omitted, causing several lost days investigating the apparently unrelated symptoms of the problem. (This was a communication failure on the part of the experiment conductor in not explaining the requirement, and on the user for not reading the user manual.) Another job developed an I/O problem resulting from attempting to combine the analyzer's Fortran I/O with the application program's assembly language I/O. It also caused the Fortran compiler to abort because the instrumented program was larger than it could handle.

3. In spite of the problems, data were acquired on the difficulty of improving test coverage. Both project programs scored surprisingly high on test coverage on the first time through;

minimal effort was put into improving these scores. However, in the case of one program, relatively little effort was needed to attain a 100% score. A high percentage of the unexecuted segments were input error detection and diagnostic code. Many of the others were exception cases.

The cost of instrumentation proved relatively inexpensive. Sizing impact on the instrumented code was somewhat more significant, ranging from 1.02 times uninstrumented code to 1.45. Timing impact, however, was major (but erratic). One job ran 8.5 times slower (21.3 versus 2.5 CPU minutes). The analyzer ran 2.5 times slower. This timing impact was considered to be the single most important disadvantage of the analyzer. The high percentage of testedness achieved caused the users to feel more secure in the reliability of their programs. Even after achieving 100% testedness, however, three more errors were detected in one of the programs!

JOVIAL Analyzer Experiment Results

Each of the JOVIAL test programs was instrumented and executed. Ongoing efforts were made, as described below, to iterate on the execution and resultant findings.

The following findings were made relative to usability in the project environment:

1. Experiment progress was slow. As with the Fortran analyzer, this was partly due to the low-priority nature of the experiment, and partly due to the extremely large number of control language errors made in setting up runs. Neither of these factors reflects on the analyzer itself.

2. Owing to the sizing impact of analyzer usage, the overlay structure for the compiler required redesign. Programs with tight memory constraints (such as overlays) will be impacted in this way.

3. As a new tool, the analyzer contained residual errors and design-caused inconveniences. All of those identified in the experiment were corrected during the experiment.

4. Review of analyzer output, and resultant test case revision to improve coverage, proved relatively easy.

Test Case → Data	Fortran Analyzer			JOVIAL Analyzer	
	Message Generator	Configuration Traceability	Fortran Analyzer	Compool Resolution Portion of JOVIAL Compiler	JOVIAL Analyzer
Program Size	133 segments (only one sub-program of 45 instrumented)	115 segments (whole program)	1493 segments (whole program)	104 segments,* (only one por-tion of compiler)	55 segments,* (whole program)
Test Coverage first pass	79%	90%	48%	71% using portion of compiler as test case;	88%
Subsequent pass	X	98% after 1 hour 100% after 2 hours	X	90% using whole compiler accep-tance test	99% after 1 hour work
Sizing Impact	X	1.02-1	1.45-1	1.1-1	1.1-1
Timing Impact	X	8.5-1	2.5-1	1-1 for whole compiler	4.8-1
Preprocessor Speed	1500 statements/CPU minute			2000 statements/CPU minute	
Number of Executable Statements per Segment	1.5	1.6	1.1	10.1	11.5

Figure 3.10   Analyzer Experiment Data Summary

Instrumentation itself was inexpensive (about 2000 statements per CPU minute). Sizing impact on the instrumented code was 1.1 times the uninstrumented version. Timing impact was more significant, 1.5 to 4.8 times. As would be expected, the sizing and timing impact were less than that for fine-grain analysis. They were also much more heavily dependent on programming style (e.g., if few GOTOs were used, there will be few labels to instrument).

Experiment Conclusions

The conclusions of the experiment were qualified as being tentative. The experiment conducted was by no means exhaustive. There was much more to learn about analyzers and their use (see Figure 3-10 for a summary of the experiment data).

1. Analyzers have value as an incremental improvement in software reliability, as well as for other reasons. The quantity of such improvement remains to be determined.
2. Fine-grain analyzers provide the most rigorous reliability improvement. They also impose the highest usage cost. Use of them should probably occur at the unit test level.
3. Coarse-grain analyzers, though less rigorous, have less cost impact. As such, they may be more useful at the system integration level.

Both analyzers need efficiency improvements to decrease the cost of use.

Four

Reliability Tool
and Technique Menu,
Management

In introducing Section 3, the circuitous path from craftsmanship to automation in software development was mentioned. Some serious questions about where we were on that path, and whether it is one that we should be moving down, were also raised.

If the traverse of that path is difficult for technologists, it is even more so for management. The manager of software development is being confronted with a series of challenges to change. How do you manage, for example, top-down programming? chief programmer teams? peer code reviews? proof of correctness? If all the implications of these technology elements are considered, each one of these techniques (if adopted) requires both a learning experience and a change in technique for the manager.

Software reliability is not the least of the forces fomenting change. As the increasing emphasis on reliability technology permeates all phases of the software life cycle, the manager must estimate, negotiate, motivate, enable, and control a highly modified technology. From decisions on system modeling in the specification phase, through use of program design languages in the design phase, into use of ana-

179

lyzers and assertion checkers in testing, to regression testing in maintenance, the manager must adopt, and adapt to, new ways of doing business.

Reliable software calls for special planning, organizational, documentation, and scheduling considerations. Each of these is dealt with in the paragraphs that follow.

REFERENCES

1. *The Mythical Man-Month,* Addison-Wesley, 1975; Brooks.

A treasury of insights into software management, drawn from practical experience on the implementation of OS/360.

2. "A Perspective on Software Development," *Proceedings of the 3rd International Conference on Software Engineering, 1978;* Hetzel.

Describes the evolution of one manager's thinking on the problems of software development. Cites "ineffective management" as the largest causative factor but observes that there is no one "main" problem.

4.1   PLANNING

4.1.1   Roadblocks to effective planning

Considering the portion of the development dollar that is typically expended on software integration and test (approaching 50% for large-scale projects), it is difficult to explain the low level of effort and scanty resources traditionally allocated to the typical reliability planning effort. The cost saving achievable from a well-planned and adequately scoped operation is difficult to measure, of course. On the other hand, the expensive consequences of poorly planned reliability efforts have undoubtedly been experienced by the vast majority of senior software designers and managers. In addition, trade journals, conference papers, and textbooks contain horror stories of the dire consequences that often ensue when test planning is neglected or delayed. There seem to be no objective reasons for the low esteem in which software reliability is held; some of the explanations or rationalizations are:

1. Integration, testing, and other reliability activities are regarded by most software developers (and their supervisors) as being far less interesting and professionally less rewarding than the analysis, design, and coding phases of the job. Reliability often becomes the training arena for less-experienced team members.

2. Naive software designers sometimes appear to believe that testing is an incidental function or even that this time *their* module will contain (at most) a few trivial errors. These superstitions may be practically unshakeable, in spite of considerable historical evidence to the contrary.

3. The reliability effort, to be effective, requires a considerable amount of advance planning, which is generally accompanied by large volumes of documentation. Documentation may well be the only task that is more detested by the "creative" software designer than either testing or program maintenance.

4. Software development supervisors are often pressured to trim budget estimates and "move up" delivery dates during the proposal and contractual negotiation phases of the project. Since the major expenditures for software reliability occur during the last stages of the effort, there is a tendency to short change testing and hope that, for once, everything will go according to schedule or that superhuman effort at the eleventh hour will effect miracles.

The foregoing list by no means covers the spectrum of roadblocks to effective reliability planning. There are any number of administrative and technical factors that might be cited. However, the objective considerations which often result in a poorly planned and executed software reliability program seem to boil down to just a few:

1. The specifications and requirements are not clearly established early in the program.

2. The impact of design changes on the reliability effort is not completely assessed before implementation is approved.

3. The software design is established before any significant consideration is given to the technical aspects and organization of reliability tasks.

4. Insufficient consideration is given to the manpower, computing time, and schedule impact of the development and usage of reliability tools.

5. Reliability documentation costs are not adequately scoped.

6. Software configuration management is not properly interfaced with the software test organization.

7. Customer interfaces and responsibilities are not clearly defined—especially with regard to buy-off criteria and conditions.

Before giving some guidelines and rule-of-thumb estimates, a rough categorical division of the planning effort is described in the following three paragraphs. Whether this division is, or is not, a natural one is left to the judgment of the reader.

4.1.2   Technical planning

Technical planning for the software reliability effort is directed toward the analysis of the performance, design, and quality assurance requirements levied on the computing system. The desired output consists of a translation or redefinition of those requirements into a minimal, but complete, set of detailed reliability requirements for the software system. Hand in hand with this analysis of requirements, the planner must assess the benefits and costs of various reliability tools and methods so that the desired quality assurance goals can be reached effectively.

In the initial stages of reliability planning, requirements analysis and trade-off studies are generally needed. The goal of this effort is to arrive at a reasonable technical approach and define a set of verification tests and performance demonstrations which will ensure that the software product works in accordance with its design criteria and meets specified performance requirements. Other sections of this guidebook address the technical aspects of performing reliability operations and describe the tools and methodologies that may be used for the task.

The reliability analyst is, unfortunately, often required to develop comprehensive plans and detail a test approach after the fact—when the quality assurance requirements are "cast in concrete" and the software architecture and design approach are already roughed out. Reliability planning should start as early in the requirements definition and preliminary design phases as possible, to ensure that proper consideration is given to the technical aspects of the task. Proper planning at this stage often effects economies that are large compared to the analysis effort expended.

4.1.3 Operations planning

Operations planning for the software reliability effort includes the definition of organizational interfaces and the resource budgeting and scheduling tasks. The roles of the development group, software test, systems test, and the quality engineering organizations must be established. Interfaces between these groups and the customer and end-user agencies may be defined by issuance of policy and procedures directives. Schedules and manpower estimates are prepared as an integral part of operations planning.

4.1.4 Logistics planning

This planning effort defines the facilities and support hardware and software tools needed to accomplish the software reliability task. When software test tools must be developed or redesigned, logistic planning interfaces with software development planning. Logistics planning and operations planning tasks are very interactive. Logistics planning must also be coordinated with overall project plans and schedules. Significant areas of interaction include hardware delivery dates, availability of subcontracted or purchased software, the phasing of equipment usage, and projections of occupancy of in-house and off-site facilities during the integration and test effort.

Although logistics planning is involved in the early stages of software tool development, the actual design and implementation of special-purpose test support software is usually handled as one of the regular tasks of the software development group or, occasionally, it is done by the software test organization.

4.1.5 Planning guidelines and cautions

The roadblocks to effective planning listed in Section 4.1.1 may be useful to the reliability planner, in spite of their generality, as a set of cautions, or precautions. Unfortunately, it is not so easy to arrive at a definitive set of positive guidelines for the perplexed planner. As in most other areas of project management and planning, direct personal experience with the software reliability process is undoubtedly the best teacher of the art of planning. Unfortunately, experience in software reliability planning and administration is often acquired very painfully.

Without direct personal experience (preferably broadly based experience over a number of projects of varying sizes and types), the software reliability analyst must resort to evaluating data and statistics gathered from other projects. If past history is to be reliably used as a guide, the models should be as close in size and technical complexity to the planned project as possible.

As a rule of thumb, software reliability activities, including module test and all subsequent integration activities, can be expected to require from 35 to 50% of the entire project software budget. The larger the project, the greater the percent that will be spent. In no case should the supervisor responsible be willing to undertake such a task for less than 25% of the project resources, including computer time. If the work statement includes extensive support for system integration, system test, and field installation and checkout, budget estimates should be revised upward accordingly. Under such constraints, even small-scale software development projects generally warrant reliability allocations of over 25% of the budget.

One of the most used and probably most effective techniques for performing any planning function is task partitioning. Using this technique, a complex task is broken up functionally into more and more detailed subtasks. Probable costs and durations of these subtasks can generally be estimated with a greater degree of confidence than would be possible for the "lumped" effort. For instance, the probability that major subtasks have been overlooked in the estimate is reduced substantially.

With an eye toward the future, the software reliability planner, the software test manager, the quality assurance manager, and the configuration management supervision are heartily encouraged to keep detailed records during the course of software test. Such data will be invaluable, both in an individual and collective sense, for future planning and proposal efforts.

REFERENCES

1.   "Viking Software Data," RADC-TR-77-168, "Flight Operations Software Plan," pp. 237–243, 1977.

Describes the form and content of the software development plan for the Viking space project software. "The true impact of the plan was that it established the basis for successfully developing a million-plus source card software system on schedule."

2.   "A Systems Approach to Computer Programs," *A Management Guide to Computer Programming,* American Data Processing, 1968; Pokorney and Mitchell.

Elementary discussion of the role of computer programs in Air Force systems management. Defines the elements of the software development process and management participation in those elements. Cites examples, some painful.

3.   *Reliable Software Through Composite Design,* Petrocelli/Charter, 1975; Myers.

Stresses modularity and design as key elements of software development. Discusses "management of design" from a structured programming point of view, listing appropriate management techniques.

4.   "Air Force Command and Control Information Processing in the 1980's: Trends in Software Technology," R-1012-PR, The Rand Corp., 1974; Kosy.

Describes the evolution and postulated future of software as seen through the perspective of command and control technology. Recommends (1) evaluating structured programming concepts, (2) expanded use of operational system simulation, and (3) software-first computer system design.

5.   "Staffing the Albatross Project," *Datamation,* Feb., 1976; Kenney.

A facetious look at the problems of staffing a tightly budgeted and scheduled project.

4.2   ORGANIZATION

Software reliability activities are not carried out in a vacuum, organizationally speaking. Depending on the size, criticality, and contractual arrangements, a wide range of organizational entities may get involved with the reliability effort. A list of these might include:

1. Software subcontractors and vendors.
2. Software subcontract management.
3. Software design.
4. Software integration.
5. Software product assurance (test).
6. Support software development.
7. Data management.
8. Software quality engineering.
9. Software configuration management.
10. System test.
11. Customer/user groups.
12. Independent software "certification" contractor.
13. Software operations and maintenance contractor.

On "small" software development projects, many of the functions will be combined, with one organization, or even some key individuals, responsible for more than one of the reliability tasks. On large projects, the communication problems obviously can be major.

Software reliability, like most other technical disciplines in an era of large-scale systems development, is both the victim and the beneficiary of sheer scale. Victim, in the sense that large-scale software brings large-scale headaches, caused by program errors that increase in number in a nonlinear ratio as the number of instructions increase; beneficiary, in that these problems have forced a more rational and analytical approach to the technology and management of the reliability effort. Whether this is a step forward or two backward from the "old" days, when one or a very few programmers designed, coded, debugged, and tested their own routines, from start to finish, is a moot point. A higher degree of organization and discipline has been forced, willy-nilly, in order to undertake larger and larger software development jobs.

This subsection discusses three of the most important organizational roles relating to the reliability function. These functions are quality assurance, product test, and configuration management. These three organizational entities have evolved to meet specific management control needs. They are likely to remain on the scene in their present form only as long as a recognized need exists for the function that they perform. Recent shifts to structured programming methods and the programming team organization may result in far-reaching changes to the roles and functions of these groups.

In the organizational structure described in the following three paragraphs, the software design/development group, product test, and the configuration management organization generally operate as three independent functional entities (as least on "large" projects). The quality assurance organization is empowered to review the performance of these three groups, to ensure that overall standards and procedures are enforced, and to certify that the end product has an acceptable level of reliability.

In addition to these purely reliability-oriented organizations, a different organizational approach, known as the chief programmer team, is also discussed.

REFERENCES

1. "Automated Techniques for Project Management and Control," *Practical Strategies for Developing Large Software Systems,* Addison-Wesley, 1975; Bratman.

Discusses the possibility of automating project management. Stresses integration of structured programming concepts with the management process. Describes a set of tools called APMIS (Automated Project Manager's Information System).

4.2.1 Software quality assurance

As the focus on software reliability increases, emphasis is placed more and more strongly on a separate organization, detached from the developmental group, to be responsible for quality and reliability-related concerns. This responsibility dichotomy is being promoted especially for large projects. Advocates have called this organizational entity *software quality assurance* (SWQA).

The broad purpose of the software-quality-assurance discipline is to assure that computer program design, code, associated documentation, and performance comply with contractual requirements. These aims are accomplished by implementing a system of controls that are applied to all phases and aspects of the software development process. While the emphasis of SWQA is on preventive measures to minimize the occurrence of deficiencies in the software product, SWQA also actively assists in promoting software quality.

SWQA brings together software control disciplines to form an organized and coordinated approach for accomplishing those controls. It is responsible for minimizing spurious control activities, and assuring the use of control disciplines.

The benefits derived from the application of SWQA disciplines are directly related to how well the SWQA disciplines are defined and put into effect; the value of those disciplines is reflected by the overall gracefulness of the development program and the ultimate quality of software operation. The ideal SWQA program will function as a low-key catalyst, keeping the organizational elements of the software development system synchronized with the total system requirements and objectives at the lowest cost in resource allocation. An insensitive SWQA system can inhibit software progress; care must be taken to achieve the proper balance between control and freedom.

How Does Software Quality Assurance Work?

The application of a software quality assurance program can be broken into three arbitrary phases—planning, development, and implementation. While the boundaries of these three phases are not distinct, it is necessary to accomplish all three to have an effective SWQA system.

The initial planning for SWQA is developed during precontract activities, where SWQA provisions are incorporated into the proposal for the software system. Integrating the provisions into the early planning assures the compatibility and effectiveness of the SWQA program, rather than including it as an "add-on" function after the software project has begun. When the software program is ready for startup, final SWQA planning is conducted. This consists of defining the SWQA tasks and methods, and developing the basic SWQA command media. An important part of this activity is the preparation of the SWQA plan.

Development of the SWQA program consists of establishing the organizational responsibilities for the SWQA tasks and selecting personnel for carrying out all tasks. This phase includes synchronizing the SWQA activities with the software program activities; it also entails setting up the working relationship between functional organizations and documenting these interfaces and operating methods with operating procedures and instructions.

Implementation encompasses all subsequent activities needed to conduct the SWQA system of controls and activities. This phase extends from the allocation of the system requirements to the software subsystem to product "buy-off" and subsequent in-field operational controls.

During the software development program, SWQA provides assessments, evaluations, and reviews of the software product. SWQA also conducts many of the actual software control functions. Specifically, the control system covered by SWQA consists of the following tasks:

1. *Planning.* Plans for SWQA are incorporated into the overall software program planning; software planning is evaluated for adequacy.
2. *Work tasking and authorization.* Cost, schedule, and resource control are evaluated for inclusion and adequacy of all elements essential to the SWQA program.
3. *Software standards.* Standards that guide the preparation of software documentation, design, code, and verification are prepared and evaluated for adequacy.
4. *Software design control and surveillance.* The software design process and design products are evaluated for conformance to requirements. Software requirements are evaluated for adequacy.
5. *Software verification.* Verification of software design is conducted and monitored for compliance with design and performance requirements, adequacy of methods used, and positive evidence of compliance.
6. *Software test control.* Software test requirements, plans, and procedures are reviewed for compatibility and adequacy; software tests are monitored for conformance with procedures.

7. *Tools and methodologies.* Special tools, techniques, and methodologies are planned, controlled, and applied to support SWQA objectives and assist in software verification.

8. *Coding control.* Coding practices are monitored and reviewed for conformance to quality standards.

9. *Reviews and audits.* The planning, preparation, and conduct of internal and formal reviews are assisted and evaluated to assure that they fulfill their intended function; formal audits are conducted to evaluate software verification results and determine readiness for delivery/acceptance.

10. *Software configuration management.* The design configuration of computer programs and all associated documents is controlled by identifying and baselining* the configurations; change control and accounting procedures are followed to assure proper implementation and visibility for software changes.

11. *Code control.* Computer program library files are established to retain the software configurations and to preclude unauthorized access or changes to controlled software; authorized changes are incorporated and the library files maintained.

12. *Computer program media control.* Storage and handling procedures are implemented to prevent degradation of software or loss of data contained on physical media and to assure the use of correct software configurations during formal testing and the delivery of a correct configuration.

13. *Discrepancy reporting and corrective action.* A system is implemented for recording, reporting, and tracking software problems and for assuring adequacy of corrective actions.

14. *Procurement control.* Provisions are established to assure that appropriate quality requirements are imposed on subcontractors and their products.

*"Baselining" is defined in Section 4.2.3.

15.   *Software acceptance.* Predetermined quality criteria must be met by the system software before it is permitted to be placed in operational status.

State of the Art in Software Quality Assurance

The trend toward a separate SWQA function has been marked in recent years, especially on complex software projects. To date, it is more often advocated than practiced; as can be seen from the references (below), that situation is changing.

REFERENCES

1.   "The Economics of Software Quality Assurance," *Proceedings of 1976 National Computer Conference;* Alberts.

Analyzes the software life cycle from an economic point of view to determine when emphasis on quality assurance techniques should be placed. Examines the effectiveness of SWQA techniques and tools (structured programming, top-down development, chief programmer teams, automated tools). Concludes that SWQA emphasis should be on "the early detection and elimination of design errors."

2.   "Implementing a Software Quality Assurance Program for the Viking Lander Flight Software," *Transactions of the Software '77 Conference;* Prudhomme.

Describes the Viking spacecraft and its mission to explore Mars. Gives a detailed description of the Viking SWQA program, which consisted of (1) design assurance, (2) configuration control, (3) verification/validation testing, and (4) failure reporting. Impacts on several Viking software functional areas are described.

3.   "The QA Role in Software Verification," *Transactions of the Software '77 Conference;* Scholten.

Stresses the total-life-cycle approach to software verification. Describes impacts of SWQA on each of those phases. Advocates a separate SWQA organization.

4.   "Software Quality Assurance for Reliable Software," *1978 Proceedings of the Annual Reliability and Maintainability Symposium;* Howley.

Defines quality software and the steps to achieve it. Describes quality tools and technologies, and advocates an integrated organizational approach to using them.

4.2.2 Product test

A product test organization is one that performs testing of programs developed outside its scope. In large projects, product test may be one function of a software quality assurance organization; on smaller projects, or where no software QA organization exists, product test may be the only part of the software organization separate from the development team.

The purpose of product test is to provide a more objective framework for testing activities. The programmer will have performed his own testing, but because of mind-set and ego problems, it may be impossible for him to ruthlessly test software he has developed. The role of the separate organization is to isolate and standardize the scope and depth of testing across project or corporate lines.

This type of testing will likely cost more than traditional methods, owing largely to the need for an additional management hierarchy. For large and medium-large projects, however, the incremental cost will not be significant.

Product test is normally made responsible for all formal software verification and validation activities. It may be assigned further responsibility in the areas of monitoring engineering development tests and module integration performed by the software development group, participate in change coordination, and provide system-level test support. It is not, however, responsible for unit or other informal tests; these remain the domain of the development group.

Product test prepares the test plan, test procedures, and test reports documents; executes the tests; and performs post-test data reduction and analysis. Problems discovered are reported to the development organization, corrected program versions are resubmitted to product test for retesting.

It is not the functions of product test that makes this concept different from traditional approaches—what product test does is what software developers have always done (or tried to do). What does make this concept different is the allocation of those functions to a separate and (hopefully) less emotionally involved group.

State of the Art in Product Test

The product test organization choice is more often one of institutional preference than of evolving trend. The history of the concept dates back several years; some companies use it extensively, others not at all.

REFERENCES

1. "An Organization for Successful Project Management," *Proceedings of the 1972 Spring Joint Computer Conference;* Smith.

Presents a software project organization emphasizing separation of responsibilities and formal checks and balances. Defines the problems plaguing software development. Proposes a development group, an integration group, and a project test group, and discusses their roles.

4.2.3   Configuration management

Configuration management is a discipline that identifies, baselines, controls, and reports changes to software products, which it refers to as configuration items.

1. *Configuration identification.* An activity that collects and defines all information which is to be controlled. The concern is with controlling the total identity and integrity of the computer program configuration item rather than its technical adequacy or its quality.
2. *Configuration baselining.* The process of officially recognizing a particular configuration with all its associated specifications and technical documentation. This action establishes that exact configuration as a control point; it then becomes a reference against which all subsequent changes must be formally accounted.
3. *Change control.* The process of evaluating, coordinating, and approving or disapproving the implementation of changes to an item that is under baseline control. The purpose of this process is to assure and expedite the implementation of needed changes and to prevent unnecessary ones.
4. *Configuration accounting.* Consists of all the activities for keeping track of the current status.

The role of configuration management is one of maintaining software stability or controlling change in an evolutionary manner. This is an essential role, given the state of the software art and the complexity of many software tasks.

The cost of configuration management varies with the degree of formality imposed and with the size of the project. Large and medium-large projects find that the relative cost of a separate and formal configuration management organization is medium-low; smaller projects probably will have to use organizationally informal techniques to keep costs within bounds.

State of the Art of Configuration Management

Configuration management is an established engineering discipline in industry, having been applied to the whole spectrum of hardware projects for several years. However, only in recent years have these disciplines been applied to software development. This avoidance resulted from a lack of understanding about how software could be controlled and how it related to hardware development. The once-prevailing attitude that programmers were an elite corps of "free spirits" also worked against putting controls on software. Eventually, the absence of such disciplines was recognized by the procuring agencies of military systems as a major source of software-related cost and schedule problems. As a result, the DoD and the military branches issued a series of standards and specifications dealing with software configuration management.

While industry is currently applying the technique to software projects, there is no generally used standard that specifically defines the methods and techniques. (Military Standard 483, found in AFSCM 375-1, is an exception.) Consequently, implementation is accomplished by borrowing the methods from one project and adapting them to the peculiarities of another. The extent to which the discipline is applied is usually determined by the contractual requirements, customer interest, and the past experiences of the project management.

How Does Configuration Management Work?

Configuration management is applied to all elements of the software product—specifications, design, documentation, listings, and so on. The components are assigned identification, and change status against that identification is maintained.

Code control usually consumes more than half of the software configuration management effort (the remainder goes into control of the design). This is because source code is quite dynamic (often modified); code is prepared in one form (high-order language) and transformed into another (executable object code); any number of object code configurations can be generated from one source, depending on the hardware configuration (target processor, emulator, test interfaces, training devices, etc.), on the application (mission, demonstration, test situation, simulation, etc.), and on the environment used to create the object code (compiler/assembler/translators, loader, link-editors, etc.). Also, code of any mode contained on physical media of any type is difficult to comprehend, therefore making it difficult to control.

A sampling of the more important methods of code control are described below.

1. *Computer program library* (CPL). In its simplest form, the CPL is both a repository for storing and processing code configurations and a means of protecting their integrity. The code's integrity is protected by isolating it from unauthorized individuals and by allowing only documented and approved changes to be incorporated. Documentation should provide a history of all changes, so that any previous configuration can be reconstructed. Code configurations should be uniquely identified, so there can be no confusion in distinguishing between them. Depending on the size, complexity, need for security, and available facilities, the CPL will vary from a simple secured storage area with manually kept records to an automated system using remote terminals, duplicate disc and magnetic tape storage, and computer-generated reports.

    "Comparator" programs, tools that identify deviations between new and baseline code, are sometimes used to police CPL updating.

2. *Code change control.* This is a system for processing all changes to software controlled by a CPL. It requires that

the requested change be fully described, coordinated with interfacing design groups, verified/retested, and approved before it is implemented.

In addition to preventing unnecessary or bad changes, the system should assure that the change is incorporated into the proper configuration in the required time frame, and that all impacts to the documentation are dealt with.

3. *Patch control.* This is a system for controlling object code changes, often called "patches." Patches are sometimes used to correct errors in the code while executing under a controlled condition (such as during verification testing); they also are used to make changes to the software in order to execute in a special environment or situation. Patches are very dangerous (since they involve changing the code at a level and in a medium which are error-prone), but sometimes they are necessary.

The medium for the patch control system is the form upon which the patch is described (in octal, hex, or binary). Each documented patch is released or published. In this manner, only approved and documented patches can be used to test software and to make changes to controlled software configurations.

Where a patch is known to be needed for a test situation beforehand, it should be included as an entry in the test procedure. Obviously, the use of patches is detrimental to long-term reliability and should be prevented when possible.

REFERENCES

1. "An Investigation of Programming Practices in Selected Air Force Projects," RADC-TR-77-182, 1977; Perry and Willmorth.

Section II.4.4 is a frank discussion of configuration management practices and failures in a large military project coded by System Development Corp. Results are quantified.

2. "Practical Experiences in Establishing Software Quality Assurance," *IEEE Symposium on Computer Software Reliability, 1973;* Keezer.

Defines configuration management in the context of software quality assurance. Cites applicable military specifications. Defines the software baseline and its role.

3.   "Modern Programming Practices Study Report," RADC-TR-77-106, 1977; Branning, Willson, Schaenzer, and Erickson.

Section 6 of this report describes the configuration management practices employed on four major programming efforts performed by Sperry Univac for the U.S. Navy. Evaluations of effectiveness are made.

4.   "Patching Is Alive and, Lamentably, Thriving in the Real-Time World," *SIGPLAN Notices,* Mar., 1978; Glass.

Defines patching, explains why it is bad and why its use is rising, and suggests techniques for minimizing or eliminating its use.

4.2.4   Chief programmer team

A *chief programmer team* is a small group of software specialists organized to do a specific project or set of tasks, such that the specialists are led by an experienced software developer and supported by a clerical person with unique software skills. Typically, the team also includes two to four other programmers of varying skill levels. The lead person is called a chief programmer, and the clerical person a librarian. The role of the librarian is to support the other team members in such essentially clerical roles as code editing, job control setup, job submission and retrieval, and project and personnel data management.

The chief programmer team is a technology-centered approach to software organization. Its value lies in the focus placed on software development, as opposed to administrative and clerical activities.

Further, the chief programmer team stresses a team rather than individual contributor approach to software. Hopefully, the sense of team responsibility among individual members is enhanced, while the ego involvement that sometimes constrains individual contributors is diminished. In this way, reliability of the resultant software should be improved. The team approach facilitates peer code review, for example, because it is team software being reviewed by the team, rather than individual software being reviewed by protaganists.

Although this approach has been used (with or without the formal name) throughout much of the history of computing on selected projects, few comparative data are available to support or reject it.

The cost of the approach lies primarily in the management adjustment necessary to introduce the new organizational methodology. As with the value, this has not been quantified.

How Does a Chief Programmer Team Work?

The chief programmer team has total technical responsibility for its project, and a large measure of management responsibility, within the team. Direction is given by the technical lead. Team members concentrate on technological tasks. Support functions, such as job control language preparation and job submittal/retrieval, are handled by the librarian. Additionally, documentation, configuration management, and data collection for management purposes are centralized in the librarian function. Interaction of technologists centers on the communally owned code, as controlled by the librarian. The focus of the team is on a particular task or set of tasks; upon completion of those tasks, the team may or may not be kept intact for other tasks.

REFERENCES

1.   "Programming as a Social Activity," *The Psychology of Computer Programming,* Van Nostrand Reinhold, 1971; Weinberg.

Discusses "egoless programming" and individual ownership of programs. Advocates the team approach to software development and reviews. Uses an anecdotal approach.

2.   "Structured Programming in a Production Programming Environment," *Proceedings of the IEEE International Conference on Reliable Software, 1975;* Baker.

Describes the chief programmer team as an element of structured programming methodology. Gives guidelines for use, and assesses experience with the technique.

3.   "The Surgical Team," *The Mythical Man-Month,* Addison-Wesley, 1975; Brooks.

Draws an analogy between chief programmer team concepts and the surgical team of the medical profession. Characterizes the individual team roles and tells how they work.

4.   "An Investigation of Programming Practices in Selected Air Force Projects," RADC-TR-77-182, 1977; Perry and Willmorth.

Section II.4.5 is a frank discussion of the successes and failures of using chief programmer teams on large military projects by System Development Corp. Suggests the notion of a "chief architect" over a hierarchy of chief programmers.

4.3 DOCUMENTATION

Documentation is the human-readable material that supplements the computer-readable program itself. As such, it includes a variety of reports and descriptions, not the least of which is the listing of the program. It is essential that this human-readable material be an accurate representation. This is easier said than done; documentation accuracy often lags behind the software it describes. Modern techniques such as word processing systems may be vital to obtaining and retaining accurate documentation.

The following discussion of software reliability documentation is keyed to the plans and procedures that are generated for U.S. government and military customers. This approach is taken because that environment has provided the most thorough and well-defined definition of what software documentation should contain. In general, government and especially military projects include documentation requirements on the same level of importance as the requirements for the software product itself.

Typically, government required software reliability documents fall into four broad categories: planning documents, administrative procedures, software test procedures/reports, and support documentation. A brief discussion of the several types of documents that might be included in each of these categories is given below. It should be kept in mind that the content and purpose of a specific document is of more interest than its "official" project name. Overlap of document content is also not unknown in the reliability business.

4.3.1 Reliability planning documents

4.3.1.1 COMPUTER PROGRAM DEVELOPMENT PLAN

The *computer program development plan* may also be known as the "software management plan." It typically provides a top-level overview of the organizational responsibilities, project phasing, and major tasks to be accomplished during the software development process. A summary of the reliability technical approach, the organizational relationships, and the top-level schedules for test and integration activities should be included in this document.

4.3.1.2 COMPUTER PROGRAM TEST PLAN

The *computer program test plan* covers planning and scheduling of formal software verification through qualification testing. If the development effort output consists of more than one identifiable computer program, the span of the test plan document usually includes formal qualification testing of the entire software portion of the total system, but normally does not include "system-level" integration and test.

4.3.1.3 FACILITIES MANAGEMENT PLAN

The facilities management aspects of a software project are principally concerned with the supporting hardware and office and laboratory facilities that will be required during code development and verification. Analysts responsible for reliability planning will usually provide inputs to the *facilities management plan,* including their specifications for computers, peripheral equipment, office and laboratory space, and on-dock and need dates for hardware and real estate.

4.3.1.4 CONFIGURATION MANAGEMENT PLAN

The *configuration management plan* is tied into reliability planning activities principally through (1) software release levels defined by degrees of testedness; (2) problem reporting and retest required after a change is made to a software test article; and (3) responsibilities for test reporting, test monitoring, and interface coordination between the developing organization and software quality engineering. The configuration management plan will also spell out the code and documentation change procedures and data required to release and maintain test input data files, test support and test tool code, and associated design specifications and user manuals. If an automated test library and/or verification data base is maintained, its management procedures may be included in, or referenced by, the configuration management plan.

200

4.3.2   Administrative procedures

Administrative procedure directives that may be of specific interest to the practitioner of software reliability include document format and release procedures, the quality assurance function, and the security and access control responsibilities if classified code, data, or documentation is involved. Since such directives are highly project- and company-dependent, nothing more is said about them here.

4.3.3   Software test procedures/reports

Software test procedures and report documents can range from informal memoranda describing low-level subroutine and unit code development tests to a coordinated scenario for a simulated operational exercise involving large numbers of people and massive amounts of equipment and processing time.

4.3.3.1   TEST PROCEDURES

Test procedures consist of a short summary of the test objectives and expected results; a definition of the test article configuration; the test setup; and any support facilities, hardware, or software that will be required to run the test. Additional information may include the test location and schedules and the test input data files and software tools to be used.

Test procedures describe the detailed process required to set up, initialize, and run the test. Post-test data reduction and analysis procedures are also spelled out, as are the expected test results and pass/ fail criteria. References are made to appropriate user documents and manuals for standard procedures. Test input data on computer-sensible media are appropriately identified and listings are appended or referenced.

4.3.3.2   TEST REPORTS

Test reports are generally not independent documents. Test procedure documents sometimes have blank spaces to record results of test runs and critical test data which will demonstrate the expected performance. For convenience, the data to be recorded are usually grouped on separate data sheets appended to the procedural material. When all the blanks are filled in and signed off by the responsible individuals, they constitute the body of the test report document. Additional summary material and an explanation or interpretation of the test results may be prepared to accompany the data.

Occasionally, the cumulative results or implications of a series of related tests must be evaluated and presented in terms of an "analysis" report. Also, nontest verification methods, such as peer code reviews or code analyzer runs, may not easily fit into a test report format. Unless the customer has a preferred format, the author of such a report should simply follow good documentation practices.

4.3.4   Support documentation

Support documentation is essential to the understanding of a software product. At minimum, it will consist of a user's manual and an operator's manual. Usually, a maintenance manual is also required. Sometimes a concept manual will be produced.

4.3.4.1   USER'S MANUAL

The *user's manual* is directed solely at the user of the software product. It describes in his language all the information needed to use the program—input format and content, job setup information, resource requirements, normal and abnormal outputs, and any other anomalies and/or operating system interfaces. The document may be tutorial (readable from cover to cover) or reference-oriented (to facilitate looking up specific facts) or both. Sometimes user's manuals are written in hierarchic fashion, where the first section is the minimal subset of information necessary to use the product, with successive levels of complexity described in subsequent sections.

4.3.4.2   OPERATOR'S MANUAL

The *operator's manual* is directed solely at the execution of the software product on the computer. It describes in the operator's language all the information needed to install, configure, and operate the program.

4.3.4.3 MAINTENANCE MANUAL

The *maintenance manual* is directed solely at the software product's inner workings. It describes in programmer's language all the information needed to maintain the program—an overview of the functions and philosophy of implementation, descriptions of the data base and its relationship to the program structure, and each element of the structure, detailing its input, output, processing, and anomalies.

It is here that the greatest difficulty arises in keeping documentation current; heavy emphasis on making the listing of the program itself serve as a focal point of the documentation, and use of automated documentation systems, can help alleviate the danger of the descriptive word not matching the software product.

4.3.4.4 CONCEPT MANUAL

The *concept manual* is usually directed solely at the early design phase of a software product. It relates customer requirements to design thinking, discussing feasibility and methods of problem solution. It is typically an expendable document, one obsoleted by subsequent implementation, one used to obtain customer approval of a method of approach. However, it can also prove useful as an introductory or high-level preface to the maintenance manual (if it is kept current).

REFERENCES

1. MIL-STD-483 (USAF), Appendix VI, 1970.
Describes the detailed form and content requirements for military software specifications. The development (Part I) specification describes requirements; the product (Part II) specification describes the completed software's internal configuration.

4.4 PREDICTION AND SCHEDULING

The management role in software reliability is more than one of planning, manning, and control. Responsiveness to changing circumstances demands understanding and agility. It is the purpose of this section to define those elements of software development which involve coping with revision to carefully conceived plans, based on analyzing task-in-process data. More than the previous sections, they rely on technological tools to improve the management process.

4.4.1   Software reliability modeling

In a statistical sense, the reliability of a piece of software is the probability that it will operated without fault (i.e., output is within specified tolerances for a specified environment) during a set time interval. A software reliability model is a mathematical model that predicts this reliability based on parameters which are previously known or evaluated during integration and test of the software. The most commonly referenced models are based on the error rate and elapsed testing time during the integration testing phase.

The rate of software error discovery is sampled over the testing time period. In addition, testing time to discovery of errors, time to fix errors, and mean time between failure (MTBF) (in some cases) are input to the model. With these inputs, the model is then used to predict the number of remaining errors, the future MTBF, and the time needed to remove the remaining errors.

The value of such modeling is not without controversy. There are those who say, for example, that measuring the mean time between failure of software makes no sense, since software does not break or wear out but instead contains only latent undiscovered errors. However, others say that such concepts are useful. For example, the models may be used to estimate errors left to correct and the effort necessary to remove them, as well as the expected future failure rate. In any case the goal of modeling is to provide management with quantitative guidelines for making decisions about software reliability and testedness. The cost of this modeling varies with the availability of valid models and is as difficult to quantify as its value.

State of the Art of Software Reliability Modeling

There is active research going on in the development and application of these models. Rome Air Development Center (U.S. Air Force), for example, is creating and testing software error models against data gathered from large-scale software development projects.

Thus far this technique is in the experimental stage and is not used industry-wide. One of the problems is that its use requires careful and complete gathering of data during testing (not after), which in turn implies integration of this technique into the overall management approach. Another problem is that modeling results to date are inconclusive.

REFERENCES

1. "Reliability Measurement During Software Development," *Proceedings of the AIAA Conference on Computers in Aerospace, 1977;* Hecht, Sturm, and Trattner.

Describes a project on which failure/success data was measured and evaluated. Cites job control statements (for the IBM 360) as a major error source (two-thirds of all failures). Performs analyses of data, and postulates future applications.

2. "A Multi-project Comparison of Software Reliability Models," *Proceedings of the AIAA Conference on Computers in Aerospace, 1977;* Sukert.

Discusses error modeling using data from a large number of projects. Evaluates different modeling techniques. Describes the Rome Air Development Center (RADC) error data bank.

3. "How to Measure Software Reliability, and How Not to . . . ," *Proceedings of the 3rd International Conference on Software Engineering, 1978;* Littlewood.

A provocative paper which suggests that (1) hardwood reliability techniques are often not applicable to software, (2) mean time between failure is an inferior measure, (3) operational usefulness is more important than error tallying, and (4) subjectivity is unavoidable in reliability analysis.

4. *Software Reliability—A Study of Large Project Reality,* North-Holland, 1978; Thayer, Lipow and Nelson.

Studies empirical software reliability data—how to collect, analyze and categorize it. Surveys available software reliability models.

4.4.2   Estimating test completion

Estimating test completion is the process of determining when testing progress is sufficient to allow the software to be used. Methodology is more often intuitive than analytical, and mostly empirical.

Knowing that it is well-nigh impossible to get *all* the errors out of a nontrivial software routine, and even more difficult (and expensive) to *prove* that no errors exist, the problem remains: "What criteria should be used to establish the end point of testing?"

Methods for estimating the end point of testing can be divided into two basic types. The first is a simple assessment of the work remaining based on the current status of the verification task and the rate at which it is being completed. The second is based on tabulating errors found during successive sampling intervals in order to make a statistical determination of the number of errors that must be eliminated. These approaches are discussed in more detail in what follows.

4.4.2.1 SIMPLE ASSESSMENT

The first approach is traditional, probably as valid as any, and relatively low in cost. It is closely tied to the deterministic criterion for establishing testedness, that of meeting all specified performance and design requirements. Simply stated, the approach is to stop testing when all quality assurance requirements have been met (all test cases successfully passed), and to estimate the occurrence of this event by noting progress in verifying requirements or passing tests. This is the only known "deterministic" criterion for establishing "testedness" of software; it makes the following assumptions:

1. The parameter "number of test cases" or "number of requirements verified" is a valid measure of test progress.
2. The difficulty of passing a test or verifying a requirement is (1) either roughly equivalent to passing any other test or verifying any other requirements, or (2) the difficulty spread is sufficiently random to assume a normal distribution.
3. The work efforts, measured over a sample interval, will either be roughly equivalent or follow a normal distribution.

Whether or not these assumptions are realistic for any given test situation is very difficult to establish. As a matter of practical utility, however, this method is so simple to apply that it is very widely used.

4.4.2.2 STATISTICAL DETERMINATION

Error-count estimation techniques make use of software reliability models (see Section 4.4.1). The cumulative error count to date is compared with estimates obtained by the modeling process. If the observed data compare favorably with the model, testing end dates may be estimated with some confidence. Unfortunately, efforts to come up with a consistently useful reliability model for software have not been an unqualified success. Thus this approach, although having more potential value, incurs both higher cost and risk than the traditional approaches.

Some ways of using the estimates are:

1. Stop testing when the rate of error discovery falls below some predetermined threshold.
2. Categorize all errors according to "criticality" and stop testing after the rate of discovery of errors of a particular criticality falls below an established threshold.
3. Embed a known number of "artificial" errors in the code and consider testing complete when a predetermined number of these errors are located (see Section 3.4.2.9).

Estimation of Errors Early in a Project

One of the most widely used estimation methods is to approximate the number of instructions in a module and assign an error probability rate based on similarity to previously developed code. Alternatively, if no historical experience applies, an error rate can be assigned based on a subjective estimate of the complexity of the module.

This method can, at best, only give a rough estimate of the overall scope and effort that will be needed. The validity of this estimate rests on the ability of the prognosticator to size and scope both his task and his error rate.

Error Estimation from Code Samples

More sophisticated error prediction techniques require that source code samples be examined for size and complexity. In some cases, complexity is related to program structure characteristics (number of DO loops, number of nonlocal variables, etc.) which have been shown to correlate with error counts. Most of the measures based on code structure characteristics have been shown to give inconsistent results in practice, since strong correlations in one code segment or language often do not carry over into another.

Another measure of complexity (by the late Maurice Halstead of Purdue University) uses the number of "mental discriminations" needed for a programmer to write a segment of code. The associated counting rules and formulas have been hypothesized to correlate strongly with the amount of time necessary to program and debug the code examined.

Estimation from Test Data

Yet another estimation process opens up during software test operations, where errors are uncovered under relatively controlled conditions. Statistics can be gathered to establish the validity of estimates of rates of test progress and errors uncovered. The manner in which this is normally done compares test results with characteristic curves to describe the cumulative error count and error discovery rates which are typical for most software test situations.

State of the Art in Estimating Test Completion

Estimating the completion of testing has been done (albeit badly!) throughout the history of computing. Stories about progress reports noting that "testing is 90% complete" being filed week after week for the same project are legion. The question is not whether to estimate test completion, but how to. There is always someone in the customer/management world who will want to know when the program is going to be ready for honest-to-goodness users.

Statistical methods of estimation are much explored in the academic world, but little used in practice. Programmer intuition and simple assessment are the overwhelming favorites (the term is used loosely!) in the workaday world.

REFERENCES

1. "The Error Hypothesis," *Elements of Software Science,* Elsevier, 1977; Halstead.*

Bases mathematical estimation of the number of software errors on "software science" algorithms. Development of these algorithms is stressed throughout the book.

2. "Program Testing and Validating," *Datamation,* July, 1968; Gruenberger.

Stresses the importance of testing, showing examples of testing specific code. Raises the question of estimating test completion; says the answer is a function of programmer experience.

3. "Calculation of Error Proneness of Computer Programs," *Proceedings of the AIAA Conference on Computers in Aerospace, 1977;* Klobert.

Expands on the work of Halstead in test completion estimation, modifying Halstead's equations. Subjects the modified equations to several tests using real project data. Obtains error count estimates accurate within 20%.

4. "Applications of a Probability-Based Model to a Code Reading Experiment," *Record of the IEEE Symposium on Computer Software Reliability, 1973;* Jelinski and Moranda.

Discusses test completion estimation via statistical calculations based on a desk check code review of a program seeded with intentional errors. Found the calculations very sensitive to the code review ground rules.

*Maurice Halstead died suddenly Jan. 8, 1979. A warm and caring obituary may be found in SIGPLAN Notices, Feb., 1979.

Five

Software Reliability Recommendations

This guidebook is intended to serve two major purposes—to lay out the whole menu of reliability technology, with concise descriptions of each menu item and references for a more thorough understanding, and to provide a selection from that menu of a set of recommended tools for particular project usage.

Neither of these purposes will be controversy-free. The menu, which has been presented in Sections 3 and 4, contains subjective as well as objective judgments about the tools being described. These recommendations go even further in ordering by preference the various tools on the menu based on those judgments!

There is value in making such judgments, however. The advocates of each of the tools in Sections 3 and 4 make strong claims for the advantage of "their" tool; some sifting and weighing of those claims played against the real world of computing is vital to bringing order out of the advocacy situation that exists.

In preparing the recommendations that follow, the goal adhered to was maximum value to the user of the guidebook, rather than maximum conformity to current reliability research trends or industry practices. This will increase the controversy among those who expect the guidebook to echo such currently popular topics as structured programming and proof-of-correctness technologies. However, it is hoped that there will be a corresponding increase in the value of the guidebook to those responsible for implementing and/or delivering reliable software under cost and schedule constraints. Of course, these recommendations are individual and subjective—the reader is encouraged to read them, question them, and form his own.

It is worth mentioning in passing that structured programming is not dealt with per se in this volume. Each of its component portions which has a bearing on software reliability is treated as a separate menu item. The reader is thus allowed to choose among SP concepts without the necessity for making a judgment about its validity as a whole.

These recommendations for software reliability must be tempered by individual judgment as to what is practical, cost effective, and suitable for the type and usage of the computer programs being developed. To make that judgment more complicated, it may be difficult to follow some of these recommendations. Guts and a missionary attitude may be necessary to gain acceptance of methods which, for example, may trade up-front cost and manpower resources against the nebulous prospect of improved code quality and reliability.

Let us also not forget that software quality cannot practicably be tested into a code segment. Without good design and high-quality code implementation practices, the best software testing can only measure the shortcomings of the product.

5.1 ORGANIZATION OF RECOMMENDATIONS

In order to make recommendations, it is necessary to distinguish between the environments in which the tools and techniques might be used. The size of the project should have a major impact on the selection process. Clearly, a small project could seldom afford the acquisition costs of tool construction or the overhead cost of a separate quality assurance organization (although the function still needs to be performed). Thus, the recommendations that follow are broken into large, medium, and small categories.

However, this raises a new dilemma—what distinguishes between these categories? For the purpose of this guidebook, that distinction will be based on the number of programmers (analysts, designers, coders, testers, maintainers) on the project. Often in the past the distinction has been made on lines of code rather than number of programmers. It is felt, however, that number of programmers more clearly correlates with such key factors as organizational complexity, number of interfaces, and (probably) even project budget. These factors may be critical in determining the reliability of the software product. Whether the number of programmers correlates with project complexity is the subject of another controversy (which will not be dealt with here.)

The definitions are: small, 5 or fewer programmers; medium, 6 to 29 programmers; large, 30 or more programmers. These numbers may be surprising to some. It is hard to believe, in a field that came into being with zero programmers in existence 25 years ago, that a single project could consume over 100 of them, and that there are many such projects. But there are!

5.2 CRITICAL SOFTWARE

In addition to project size, it is necessary to distinguish (in the reliability world) between critical and noncritical software. Critical software must be subjected to unusually rigorous reliability constraints in order to be certain that it does not fail. Critical software is usually associated with processing components that are "embedded" in larger systems performing functions defined as critical. The critical classification for software would include at least programs that impact:

1. Personnel or public safety.
2. Equipment safety.
3. Environmental quality.
4. Military readiness or government effectiveness.
5. Data, communications, or physical security.

The empirical criterion for evaluating the degree of criticality of a software product, however, remains a simple one: How much is the customer willing to pay for a sound design and freedom from software errors?

The unique requirements of critical software are best dealt with by referring to the "reliability critical" column of Table 5.2.

5.3 RECOMMENDATIONS

The recommendations that follow are presented in tabular form. The first, Table 5.1, lists all tools regardless of type of methodology in decreasing order from "most valuable" to "least valuable." A separate listing contains those not rankable by those criteria.

In addition, a cost estimate (covering both acquisition and usage) is given for each tool, with numbers for large, medium and small projects. The numbers assigned to values and costs are on a scale of 10 (highest) to 0 (lowest), and are unit-free, being used merely for ordering. No attempt to quantify or compare value/cost numbers should be made. Table 5.1 may be used for a quick-look evaluation of a particular tool.

The second Table, 5.2, presents an alternative layout of the same tools. In this case the tools are grouped under the phase of software development to which they apply, in the same order in which they appear in Sections 3 and 4 of the guidebook. Each tool is rated as to its value in four different software project environments—traditional (what has been in the past), cost-conservative (those which cannot afford extra emphasis on reliability), reliability emphasized (those where reliability's importance in life-cycle considerations is stressed), and reliability critical (those where software success is in some sense a life-and-death matter). Users of this guidebook who have a particular project in mind are encouraged to use it at any of these levels which they find useful:

1. Using Sections 3 and 4 and their references to gain an in-depth understanding of reliability technology prior to defining an approach.
2. Using the menu of Sections 3 and 4 to become quickly familiar with the totality of reliability technology, defining a reliability approach from the knowledge so gained.
3. Using Tables 5.1 and 5.2 to define a reliability program for a specific project, referring to Sections 3 and 4 for supporting rationale where desired.

TABLE 5.1

Ranking of software reliability technological methodologies for use in production environment

Methodology	Type	Description	Value	Cost (L,M,S[a])	Ref.
Modular programming	Implementation	Appropriate to all types of programs. Contributes to program structure, readability, maintainability. Only difficulty is in choosing how to modularize.	10	0,0,0	3.3.2
Preventive maintenance	Maintenance	Programming to make maintenance easier. Removes potential for maintenance errors.	9	1,1,1	3.5.1
Error reporting	Maintenance	Recording and tracking error status. Essential to avoid neglect of errors.	9	2,2,2	3.5.4
Regression testing	Maintenance	Essential in maintenance environment for inhibiting error regeneration. Mildly expensive to build initial set of tests.	9	3,3,3	3.5.3
Design reviews	Design	Team approach to elimination of design errors. Effective if skilled people selected as reviewers. Formal reviews costly, for small projects.	9	3,5,7	3.2.2
Source language debug	Checkout	Allows programmer to preplan debug process, and debug in his own language. Expensive to obtain tools if unavailable.	9	5,6,9	3.4.2.1
Desk checking	Checkout	Vital for mathematically oriented problems. Necessary in most other debugging situations.	9	5,5,5	3.4.1.1
Peer code review	Checkout	Highly effective error detection. Tedious and expensive to perform.	9	7,7,7	3.4.1.2
Change review	Maintenance	Approval method for maintenance changes. Inhibits change-caused errors.	8	1,1,1	3.5.2
Acceptance testing	Checkout	Formal process with customer approval rights.	8	2,2,2	3.3.3

215

Methodology	Type	Description	Value	Cost (L,M,Sᵃ)	Ref.
Top-down design	Design	An effective way of enabling understanding of a total system and breaking it down into manageable pieces. Only difficulty is in identifying the "top."	7	0,0,0	3.2.1.1
Data structure design	Design	Good way of breaking up data-structure-oriented systems.	7	0,0,0	3.2.1.2
Program design language	Design	Relatively new concept. Beginning to replace flowcharting. Easier to produce and maintain.	7	1,1,1	3.2.3.2
Test coverage analyzer	Checkout	Measures effectiveness of test cases. Good way to see how testing can be improved. Expensive to obtain if unavailable.	6	3,6,9	3.4.2.2
Assertion checker	Checkout	Early-warning detection of certain classes of errors. Expensive to obtain if unavailable.	6	3,6,9	3.4.2.3
Bottom-up programming	Implementation	Traditional code/test/integrate approach. Promotes "build-ing-block" construction approach. Integration can be a serious problem.	5	0,0,0	3.3.1
Top-down programming	Implementation	Eliminates integration phase. New method, incurs training costs. Requires research for best usage in large project environment.	5	3,2,1	3.3.1
HIPO	Design	Effective method of combining function and data flow in a design representation. Good high-level overview.	5	2,2,2	3.2.3.4
Interactive debug	Checkout	Effective if necessary support tools available. Speeds debug efforts. Caution needed in use.	5	2,4,6	3.4.2.8
Flowcharts	Design	Most frequently used design representation. Under attack for clumsiness. Difficult to modify.	4	2,2,2	3.2.3.1
Structural analysis	Checkout	Effective for detection of certain types of errors. Expensive if automated tool unavailable.	4	5,5,5	3.4.1.3
Automated design checking	Design	New method of design consistency verification. Costly-to-build tool. Value not well established.	3	4,6,8	3.2.4
Foreign debug	Checkout	Combines peer code review and product test with noncoder debug. Appears to add little to the first two concepts.	2	2,2,2	3.4.2.10

Methodology	Type	Description	Value	Cost (L,M,S[a])	Ref.
Intentional failure	Checkout	Methodology borrowed from other disciplines. Appropriateness to software questionable.	2	2,2,2	3.4.2.9
Requirements/spec language	Requirements	Relatively new concept. Little used in practice. Value not well established, and questionable.	1	2,2,2	3.1.1
Symbolic execution	Checkout	Conceptually promising but with serious flaws in practice. Considerable research underway.	1	5,7,9	3.4.2.11
Proof of correctness	Checkout (also design)	Complex methodology, not yet effective for project software except small, critical areas. Considerable research in process.	1	9,9,9	3.4.1.4
Difficult to rank due to specific applicabilities					
Decision tables	Design	For logic-oriented programs or portions of programs, it is a natural representation. Otherwise, method seems inappropriate.		2,2,2	3.2.3.2
Test driver	Checkout	Essential technique for bottom-up programming. Small added cost for throwaway code.		2,2,2	3.4.2.4
Test data generator	Checkout	Effective if (1) program requires lots of input, (2) test data are of high quality. Somewhat expensive to obtain if unavailable.		3,5,7	3.4.2.6
Standardized testing	Checkout	Extremely effective if available. For most applications, not meaningful.		4,5,6	3.4.2.7
Fault-tolerant software	Implementation	For critical software, is essential. Otherwise, cost is too high.		5,5,5	3.3.3
Mathematical checker	Checkout	Important for mathematically oriented problems. Expensive to obtain if unavailable.		5,7,9	3.4.2.12
System modeling, simulation	Requirements	For complex and unusual applications, may be essential. Otherwise, cost may override value.		7,8,9	3.1.2
Environment simulator	Checkout	For software embedded in more complex and expensive or critical systems. Cost exceeds benefits elsewhere.		9,9,9	3.4.2.5

[a]L, large; M, medium; S, small.

217

TABLE 5.2

Recommended software reliability usage[a]

Methodology	Type of Project			
	Traditional (what has been)	Cost conservative	Reliability emphasized	Reliability critical
Requirements/specifications				
Requirements/specifications language			EXP	EXP
System modeling and simulation	OCC		CRIT	CRIT
Design				
Top-down design	OCC	APROP	APROP	APROP
Data structure design		APROP	APROP	APROP
Design review	APROP	APROP	ALWAYS	ALWAYS
Flowcharts	ALWAYS	OCC	OCC	OCC
Decision tables	APROP	APROP	APROP	APROP
Program design languages		APROP	APROP	APROP
HIPO			APROP	APROP
Automated design checking		AV	AV	APROP
Implementation				
Top-down programming	OCC	EXP	EXP	EXP
Bottom-up programming	ALWAYS	APROP	APROP	APROP
Modular programming	ALWAYS	ALWAYS	ALWAYS	ALWAYS
Fault-tolerant software	OCC		APROP	ALWAYS
Checkout				
Desk checking	APROP	APROP	ALWAYS	ALWAYS
Peer code review	OCC		CRIT	ALWAYS
Structural analysis			AV	CRIT
Proof of correctness				
Source language debug	AV	AV	ALWAYS (large); AV (med., small)	ALWAYS (large, med.); AV (small)
Test coverage analyzer			AV	ALWAYS (large, med.); AV (small)

[a]When to use: blank, seldom if ever. OCC, occasionally. AV, if available; don't procure. EXP, only if experienced with. CRIT, critical areas only; procure if necessary. APROP, wherever appropriate; procure if necessary. ALWAYS, always; procure if necessary. Project size: large, 30 or more programmers; medium, 6 to 29, small, 5 or less.

Methodology	Type of Project			
	Traditional (what has been)	Cost conservative	Reliability emphasized	Reliability critical
Assertion checker			AV	ALWAYS (large, med.); AV (small)
Test driver	ALWAYS	APROP	APROP	APROP
Environment simulator	APROP	APROP	APROP	APROP
Test data generator	OCC	AV	AV	AV
Standardized testing	AV	AV	AV	APROP (large); AV (med., small)
Interactive debug	AV	AV	AV	AV
Intentional failure				
Foreign debug				
Symbolic execution				
Mathematical checker			AV	AV
Acceptance testing	APROP	APROP	ALWAYS	ALWAYS
Maintenance				
Preventive maintenance	APROP	ALWAYS	ALWAYS	ALWAYS
Change review	APROP	APROP	ALWAYS	ALWAYS
Regression testing	AV	ALWAYS	ALWAYS	ALWAYS
Error reporting	OCC	APROP	ALWAYS	ALWAYS
Management				
Quality assurance organization[b]	OCC (large only)	OCC (large, med. only)	ALWAYS (large, med. only)	ALWAYS
Product test organization	OCC		ALWAYS (large only)	ALWAYS
Configuration management organization[b]	ALWAYS (large, med. only)	ALWAYS (large, med. only)	ALWAYS (large, med. only)	ALWAYS
Chief programmer team	OCC	EXP (small only)	ALWAYS (small only)	ALWAYS (small only)
Test plans/procedures/ reports	ALWAYS (large, med. only)	ALWAYS (large, med. only)	ALWAYS	ALWAYS
Software reliability modeling				APROP
Estimating test completion			EXP	EXP

[b]As a separate organization; the function must be performed in all cases.

5.4 EXAMPLE USE OF RECOMMENDATIONS

A sample meal from the menu of reliability technology can be obtained from Table 5.2. Given the type of project you are concerned with, read down the column of interest to see which techniques are recommended as appropriate. The footnotes to the table explain all cryptic terminology. Some examples are given below.

5.4.1 Cost-conservative example

You work for the city of Scenic, Kansas, and you have been asked to construct a software system to extract from U.S. government census data tapes a graphical overview of sections of the city versus income level. The output of your program will be a map of the city with highest income areas shaded and lowest income areas blank.

Because of the nature of the project, and because Scenic's budget is always in a critical state, you realistically appraise your project as cost-conservative. Certainly nothing analogous to life-or-death decisions will be made based on program results. (In fact, you suspect that the program will be used surreptitiously for political fund-raising activities.)

Your shopping trip through the menu of software reliability techniques, then, is fairly quick. You elect to use data structure design rather than top-down, because the format of the census tapes and the graphic output control the design of the program. You decide to use a program design language because you hate flowcharts, and HIPO for a system overview because you want to try it out. You plan a critical design review but not a preliminary one. No automated tools are available, and you do not plan to use any. You elect to program top-down and modular, after first defining some bottom-up building blocks. You will desk check results whenever necessary, including some sampling techniques to see if the graphic output is reasonable (fortunately, your intuition is also working for you here—as a long-time Scenic resident, you think you know where the city's big money is). You will, of course, use preventive maintenance techniques. And since your project is small, no organizational additives are needed.

5.4.2 Reliability emphasized example

Having received the completed income-level program, your pleased management assigns you to a similar project requiring you to plot criminal incidents versus areas of the city. The output of the program will be used to establish police patrols in a new pattern designed to concentrate on areas of known criminal activity. Now, you perceive, reliability is somewhat more important than in your previous assignment. For one thing, you'd hate to think that the police were erroneously concentrating their patrols on the Scenic cemetery northwest of town, when you know that Scenic's Tavern Row is probably where they belong. For another, there's always the potential of a citizen lawsuit if police protection is perceived to be inadequate, and a poorly verified program might be the grounds for such a case.

As a result, you declare your program to be "reliability emphasized" and shop from a different column on the chart. In addition to the techniques you previously employed, you add a preliminary design review, inviting the chief of police to participate in your early thinking on system design and the requirements it satisfies; considerably more thorough desk checking; a peer code review of critical parts of the program; a formal acceptance test; a change review and error reporting process during maintenance; a chief programmer team, with a backup programmer and a clerk/librarian to help out; and you utilize a well-defined and reviewed set of test documents.

5.4.3 Reliability critical example

Scenic has been selected as the site of an experimental rapid-transit people-mover system, and you are chosen to head a team of 20 programmers building the main control system and the on-board vehicle acceleration–deceleration systems. Because people will be riding around on your computer-controlled system, its reliability becomes critical. Erratic vehicular behavior might result in serious injuries or death. Your choices are now made from the rightmost column of Table 5.2, and your project is now categorized as medium in size.

One of the members of your newly formed team has a Ph.D. in computer science and a couple of years' experience at a DoD "think-tank" company. Because of his background and experience, you elect to use some new technology which you might otherwise have ignored. In addition, his contacts make available certain reliability tools to which you previously had no access. Your reliability technology now changes considerably.

You elect to use a requirements/specifications language, one compatible with the modeling language via which you intend to simulate system activity. You decide to use a top-down rather than a data structure design, since function rather than data appears to be the key to system design. Your design will now be subjected to the review of an available automated design checker. You add fault-tolerance concepts to your software implementation, and peer-code-review all segments of code. You buy a source language debug augmentation to your compiler (smug in the knowledge that now it will be available for all your other projects), and at the same time you buy a test coverage analyzer and assertion checker package off the shelf from your Ph.D's former employer. Your design simulation is to evolve into an environment simulator for test support. You split off part of your team into a product test group, solely responsible for test planning, execution, and documentation; and another part into a configuration management group. Your management assigns a quality assurance representative to your project, and his first responsibility is to bless these plans.

With an appropriate set of tools, and some good organizational checks and balances, you see the basis for a sound and reliable system implementation.

5.5   THE ROLE OF VALUE JUDGMENTS

There is a legitimate question as to the value of this section of this guidebook. Given sufficient facts to understand all the concepts defined in this guidebook, why should you the reader be presented with value judgments on top of all the other information you have absorbed? Especially when those value judgments are acknowledged to be controversial, is it not presumptuous to inject one person's opinions into an already tumultuous milieu?

The rationale that counters those arguments is simple: value judgments are vital. They are being made constantly, and they will continue to be made. Better that they are made out of a broadly knowledgeable viewpoint than out of a narrow advocacy viewpoint. If this guidebook is to define that broad viewpoint, there is even an implied obligation to bring that broad viewpoint into useful focus.

So argue, if you will, the specific value judgments made. But do not argue the need for them. In fact, counter the value judgments presented here with some of your own.

As an example of the ongoing and immediate need for value judgments, consider the following example situations. It is specifically to these situations and to these people that this section addresses itself.

5.5.1   The consultant and value judgments

Suppose that you are a consultant, hired by Company XYZ to recommend a software reliability program in support of project ABC. Armed with your knowledge of the breadth of software reliability techniques, you investigate the status quo at XYZ/ABC to determine what technologies are most readily introduced into the existing environment. At the conclusion of the investigation, you recommend a program of reliability techniques to augment or change the traditional XYZ methodology. Value judgments are vital to the process of selecting a workable program. No matter how promising you might find proof-of-correctness techniques, for example, you decide you would be ill-advised to recommend that to XYZ/ABC if their project is due for completion in the next five years and/or if their personnel are largely unsophisticated in their ability to employ complex new technologies.

Value judgments, in fact, are the very substance of what you have been hired to provide.

5.5.2   The software quality assurance manager and value judgments

Suppose, now, that you are a middle manager at Company RST and your assignment is software quality assurance. Your task is to allocate your budget and your personnel to cover the six software projects that RST is currently involved in. Do you concentrate on configuration management and other control-oriented technologies? Do you stress the product test philosophy, and assign your personnel to test generation and execution? Do you emphasize verification tools, to aid the development organizations themselves in producing better code? Again, your business is value judgments. If you plunge your resources into test coverage analyzers, for example, there may not be money and people available for broad coverage of design and peer code reviews (or vice versa).

Value judgments are an essential part of the performance of your job.

5.5.3   The software researcher and value judgments

Suppose that you have made a personal decision not to tell others what to do, and as a result you have rejected both the consultant and the management path as a career choice. Instead, owing to your advanced software skills, you have chosen to be a software research technologist.

Your first task is to pick a promising area for future research. Do you concentrate on symbolic execution because of its long-term promise, or assertion checkers because of their immediate applicability? Again, your very first decision is one involving value judgments.

There is, in fact, no way in the workaday world of computing to avoid making value judgments. As you investigate your choice of research projects further, you begin to feel even more strongly about the matter. Some avenues of possible research are obviously not promising, and yet some of your colleagues continue to pursue them. You begin to see that value judgments are not only vital, but that otherwise brilliant people are wasting their time due to inability to make them.

5.5.4   Background for these value judgments

Given that value judgments are vital. Given that it is legitimate for this guidebook to make them. The question then arises, what is the underlying viewpoint of this particular set of value judgments? After all, even the most objective of value judgments are still essentially subjective; and to understand the prejudices of the judgments, you need to understand the prejudices of the judger.

These value judgments emerge from 25 years of experience in the specification, design, development, test, and maintenance of software. The experience has been partly commercial data processing applications, partly scientific applications, and partly systems programming (especially compilers). The environment for that experience has been largely aerospace corporations, with a dash of the academic world thrown in. Blended into that experience and environment has been a heavy exposure to software research and advanced development activities.

The window for this particular set of value judgments, then, is that of the experienced and skilled software craftsman, not that of a manager and not that of an academician. The main purpose of this paragraph is to acknowledge that those other windows produce a different set of value judgments—and to recommend that the reader form his/her own!

Six

Software Reliability
Case Histories

The preceding sections of this guidebook describe an abstract "what could be" of hopefully useful software reliability techniques. It is the purpose of this section to describe "what is" in the reliability world of a few selected corporations. They are referred to herein as Company A, Company B, and Company C.

6.1 COMPANY A

In support of its Department of Defense project programs and research and development activities, Company A has undertaken a wide variety of software development activities. Reliability efforts are an important part of those tasks, both in practice and in contractual specifications.

6.1.1 State of the art in applications

The nature of Company A project reliability activities is largely determined by the project contract. A software development plan may or may not be contractually required, but it is usually developed and includes the various types of software reliability efforts to be performed. These typically will include:

1. Software development checkout (bottom-up; unit test).
2. Integration testing.
3. Formal testing (performed by product test organization).
4. Acceptance testing (at the computer program level).
5. Acceptance testing (at the system level).

Since the latter several items are formally required, they are defined in a project requirements specification. Formal test documentation procedures and reports are controlled by military standards defined in the project contract. Usually, the reliability efforts performed in all stages of the software development process are requirements-driven. One problem of reliability efforts in this environment is that, owing to schedule deadlines, the testing organizations are forced to compress testing against a milestone date and at times testing must be prioritized—important requirements will get tested and lesser ones may or may not be.

Following the development and formal testing, regression testing is used to maintain stability in the existing code during further development or maintenance. Regression testing is that series of tests run once a program has been released and subsequently modified. The regression tests are often a subset of the original tests and are run to ensure that no new errors have been introduced into the modified program.

The basic technique of testing is supplemented on the project by various software reviews. The preliminary design review (PDR) is a formal review conducted with the military customer to ensure that initial software design satisfies the software requirements. The critical design review (CDR), again conducted with the customer, ensures that the final design is adequate. In each case the formal customer reviews may be preceded by informal in-house reviews.

Other techniques have been employed less consistently, usually on an individual, project-by-project basis. Instruction-level simulation has been used to provide early software development test capability. In addition, peer code review has been used to try to eliminate errors prior to testing.

6.1.2   Research and advanced development

Company A efforts in the research and development (R & D) area of reliability have concentrated on the development of and experimentation with analyzer tools (see Section 3.4.2.2). The Fortran analyzer program constructed by the National Bureau of Standards was obtained from NBS, converted to run on the IBM 360/370 while processing Fortran IV, and made available for project usage. Additionally, an experiment to assess the value and cost of using the analyzer was conducted in a project environment. (See also Section 3.6.2, which describes the results of this experiment.)

Another analyzer was constructed in-house to operate on the 360/370 and process JOVIAL J3. As with the Fortran analyzer, an experiment using the analyzer was conducted in a project environment. The project was a significant military aircraft still undergoing development and predelivery flight testing. On-board computers play an essential aircraft mission role, especially in radar data processing and interaircraft communication.

Both analyzers were then released for general project usage. Owing to schedule constraints and lack of user familiarity, they are seldom used.

6.2   COMPANY B

As a large and prominent software house, Company B is especially interested in software reliability efforts.

6.2.1   State of the art in applications

The degree of reliability tasking on Company B-produced software is dictated either by company policy (in the case of national products) or by customer requirements. Most nonnational products can be classified as a production business system or a scientific application. Reliability activities will be discussed for each of these categories.

For national products, policy states that the product will undergo developmental testing which will show by a test plan and supporting evidence that the functional capabilities have been exercised. An alpha test is required, which may consist of an independent audit of the developmental testing (with changes as appropriate), or will be a thorough development team independent activity. The final step is to submit the product and its user documentation to a beta test. This test is intended to assess the usefulness of the product in its intended market environment. The quality assurance manager has responsibility for maintaining product integrity during each step of the process.

For a production business system run on Company B computers, reliability activities are controlled and monitored by computer operations production planning. For a business program to be certified as being in a production status, it must undergo a series of steps. The nature of a business program allows the functional specification to serve as the basis for testing. An initial step in testing a business program is to make sure that each report is being produced correctly. Once a program completes its developmental testing, it then begins processing production data. When the program can process a specified number of production cycles successfully, it is declared "certified" for production.

For scientific applications, the degree of reliability varies due to the following:

1. Criticality of the results.
2. Cost of producing the results.
3. Ability to tolerate errors (i.e., what is the cost of an error?).

For critical applications, activities have included:

1. Detailed test planning.
2. Test monitoring programs.
3. Structured test data.
4. Desk checking.

For less critical applications, the client's desires and the analyst's expertise dictate the level of reliability activities.

6.2.2   Advanced development

Company B is experimenting with two advanced reliability tools:
(1) MVA (manual verification algorithm) and (2) MPPS (machine
processable program specifications). MVA is a derivative of symbolic
execution (Section 3.4.2.11), and MPPS is a form of assertion checker
(Section 3.4.2.3).

6.2.2.1   MANUAL VERIFICATION ALGORITHM

MVA is seen as a generalization and formalization of desk checking. It is performed as a manual symbolic execution via a set of preprinted forms called MVAGRAMs on which are recorded the sequence
of computational states as the program executes.

MVA is considered to be potentially useful for small complex
computational segments which are required to have a high degree of
reliability. It works as follows. The user chooses some abstract data
as input to the program segment to be verified. For example, suppose that "X" is the name of an input variable, and the symbolic
constant "A" is chosen to be the initial value of X. Further, suppose
that A is to be an even integer. This fact may be represented by the
symbolic assertion EVEN(A). The target segment is now executed
using this abstract (or symbolic) data constant, A. The behavior to
be observed will correspond to all behaviors possible for a given input
which is an even integer.

The necessary manual bookkeeping is handled via the preprinted
forms, which are of varying widths and overlay each other.

MVA has only been applied to small test cases to date.

6.2.2.2   MACHINE-PROCESSABLE PROGRAM SPECIFICATIONS

MPPS is a development of the assertion checker concept. It is a
language (or notation) with which one can make rigorous, formalized
statements that specify the intent of a computational segment.

MPPS works as follows: MPPS assertions are embedded in the
target program. During production runs these assertions become

231

comments. During checkout the MPPS preprocessor "compiles" the MPPS into "specification code" which analyzes the state of the computation and produces an interrupt if the program has deviated from its specification.

The MPPS concept is currently in development and is still limited to a narrow range of problems.

6.3   COMPANY C

Company C is a large manufacturing company for which software activities are diverse, ranging from simulators to real-time manufacturing support systems to advanced concepts development in support of new products. No one can really summarize software reliability as practiced in this diverse environment. The material that follows is from selected areas of activity.

6.3.1   State of the art in applications

6.3.1.1   SIMULATION CENTER

The simulation center contains the components necessary to conduct Company C end-product real-time simulation, with man and/or special equipment in the loop. These components include digital and hybrid-analog computers, mockups with instrument displays, computer-generated CRT displays, visual displays, a software library, and an experienced simulation staff.

In this environment, reliability technique usage is:

Technique	Degree of use
Desk checking	Always
Design reviews	Occasionally
Interactive debug	Frequently
Peer code review	As needed
Source language debug	Occasionally

Go ahead was recently given for the development of a Company C designed rapid-transit system. This system will be strongly dependent upon computer hardware and software for its operation and will be developed with stringent reliability standards. Judging by past decisions, computing elements (both hardware and software) will probably be subcontracted to outside firms.

A specific software verification approach has not yet been formulated. Work is under way to develop and document an overall software management plan that can be used to identify the Company C subcontractor interface. Development of this plan will include a verification approach strategy to include, at minimum, top-down/structured design and programming principles. Design reviews with Company C participation, and a formalized acceptance test process, will be used to measure subcontractor performance.

6.4   CASE HISTORY CONCLUSIONS

The case histories given here present a thin and spotty view of the software reliability state of the art as it is practiced in the industrial, "real-world" environment. Nevertheless, some tentative conclusions may be drawn.

There is little consistency, either intracompany or extracompany, to software reliability practices. Some companies are moving toward "modern programming practices" such as elements of structural programming, while others are not. The approach to new technologies is frequently evolutionary and decided at the project level. Therefore, different projects within a company may use different technologies to different degrees. It is possible to find many companies and many projects using the software reliability techniques used 10 years ago. Interest in new technologies appears to be strong (as is shown by the research and development activities) but is not commonly translated into application developmental action.

Perhaps it is not too surprising that in a world still dominated by the Fortran and COBOL languages, considered obsolete by some 10 years ago, the movement toward new software reliability technologies is slow and erratic. The early statements in this guidebook to the effect that software reliability has been a neglected field thus may continue, unfortunately, to be accurate into the future in the industrial computing environment.

Seven

Bibliography

References and bibliography for this guidebook are largely found attached to the section describing a particular methodology, rather than gathered here. What follows, therefore, is a selected few references in the software reliability field which are so comprehensive and recent that a software technologist should be aware of them.

Advanced Material

1. *Proceedings of 1975 IEEE International Conference on Reliable Software.*

A collection of papers on a diverse set of reliability topics.

2. "Findings and Recommendations of the Joint Logistics Commanders Software Reliability Group" (SRWG Report), Nov., 1975.

Discussions of software reliability seen from a military perspective.

Intermediate Material

1. RADC-TR-74-300, Structured Programming Series, Vol. 15 (Validation and Verification Study), May, 1975.

An overview of reliability technology, seen from the perspective of structured programming.

2. *Software Reliability Principles and Practices,* Wiley–Interscience, 1976; Myers.

Defines principles and practices that will lead to more reliable software; stresses testing and design.

3. *Program Style, Design, Efficiency, Debugging and Testing,* Prentice-Hall, 1974; Van Tassel.

Compilation of "programming lore" derived from software experience.

4. "Program Testing," special issue of the IEEE Journal, *Computer,* Apr., 1978.

A collection of articles that represents a contemporary status report on software testing methodologies. Authors include Huang, King, and Miller.

General

And, as a warning of what will happen if reliability principles are ignored:

1. *The Universal Elixir, and Other Computing Projects Which Failed,* Computing Trends, 1977; Glass.

Recounts computing "horror stories" about projects that did not turn out as intended. Uses an anecdotal, humorous approach.

Index